MURDER AND THE MOVIES

MURDER AND THE MOVIES

DAVID THOMSON

Yale UNIVERSITY PRESS

New Haven & London

Yale University Press books may be purchased in quantity for educational,
business, or promotional use. For information, please e-mail
sales.press@yale.edu (U.S. office) or sales@yaleup.co.uk (U.K. office).

Set in Janson Roman and Felix Titling types by
Integrated Publishing Solutions.
Printed in the United States of America.

Library of Congress Control Number: 2019948577
ISBN 978-0-300-22001-8 (hardcover : alk. paper)

A catalogue record for this book is available from the British Library.

This paper meets the requirements of ANSI/NISO Z39.48-1992
(Permanence of Paper).

10 9 8 7 6 5 4 3 2 1

For Kate

We Were Sitting There Alone

Lady Macduff: Sirrah, your father is dead. And what will you do now? How will you live?
Son: As birds do, mother.

—*Macbeth*, Act IV, Scene II

If history has taught us anything . . . you can kill anyone.

—MICHAEL in *The Godfather, Part II*

It is the custom on the stage, in all good murderous melodramas, to present the tragic and the comic scenes, in as regular alternation, as the layers of red and white in a streaky side of bacon.

—CHARLES DICKENS, *Oliver Twist*

There is no point in using death to simplify ourselves.

—JOHN BERGER, *and our faces, my heart, brief as photos* (1984)

CONTENTS

CONTENTS

IN *OZARK*

We like to think we're decent people, the way you try to be, but there we were, counting our fingers to recall how many characters had been murdered in the first season of *Ozark*.

I am talking about entertainment, some fun at the end of the day—and *Ozark* was a hit show. So do we absorb these spectacular killings to have a good time? Take away murder, would the show register? Does its fun allay the tread of death on our stairs?

"Well, there was Bruce," Lucy began, "wasn't that his name? Marty's partner."

"Plus Bruce's woman," I added. "Wife or lover, I'm not sure which."

"They were both dissolved in acid, weren't they? Imagine that." She shuddered.

I think we were happy.

"And Wendy's lover," I said—it was a contest now. "I don't

recall his name. But I can hear the thump as his body landed on the sidewalk."

"Oh yes!" she said—eager in her gentleness. "Tossed off the building! What floor was it? The twentieth?"

"It may have been higher—it was in Chicago." He would have been alive coming down.

We were hurrying by then, in a quiz game. Of course, Dell was offed, as well as Dell's bodyguard, both taken out so swiftly. But with a rush of clarity or release, if only because Dell had seemed to be in charge of the game, immaculate, suave and sinister. But if Dell went, wasn't anyone vulnerable?

There was Bobby Dean, the nasty boss at The Lickety Splitz strip bar. And Mason's wife—that was regrettable because she must have been killed soon after having her baby. Then there was Garcia, the man from the cartel who delivered the money in a van—absurd quantities of cash so that Marty and Wendy had to stay up all night packing it in the walls of their home. No one ever said *Ozark* was credible, except for every hour at a time.

"And the brothers," she said. "Russ and what's his name, electrocuted, burning in the dark. I couldn't watch that."

"Right," I said, "the blood seemed to boil out of them. I wonder, is that what happens in electrocution?"

"They'd know, wouldn't they, the writers? It was probably researched." We pondered the iniquity of it, and our status as connoisseurs.

She began again. "And I think there was someone called Louis.

I remember the name, but I don't know who he was or how he was killed."

"Poor Louis," I said, hoping to be ironic. "That's eleven." I had been keeping notes. And this was just the first season.

Amazing, we agreed, while understanding that perhaps the most remarkable thing was how we—decent people trying to do better—had been so attached to this Jacobean slaughter in Missouri. Ten nights in a row, we watched two episodes back to back, rationing ourselves with its first two seasons, waiting for the third. And if we sometimes felt we had to look away, still we watched. If we couldn't follow the tortuous story, we held on in delicious desperation. Because we didn't want it to end. We'd have taken a few more murders, I think; we know that's what the show does.

You see, *Ozark* is very good.

In saying that, I'm thinking of what is called the concept (created by Bill Dubuque and Mark Williams): of how Marty Byrde (Jason Bateman), a financial adviser in Chicago, gets in such trouble with the cartel that he has to retreat to Ozark country in Missouri, with his wife Wendy and their two children, Charlotte and Jonah, and get into the frenzied business of laundering immense sums of cartel cash. It's a story of a family trying to stay a family, swept away on the flood of money and drawn to the point of murder, watching it, beholding it, and doing it. And of how the endlessly resourceful Marty becomes stunned by the compromises and the confusion of his terrible life, until his attempt at kindness withers, but sweet-smiling Wendy (Laura Linney) emerges as the polite monster who may drag the family to safety.

Not that safety is a sure prospect in this Ozark country. But the peril is so well shaped and written, that's what the critic can say. And it is acted with that brimming American fluency that prefers acting to being—isn't that our last way of getting through, of staying "in character" or coherent when one's life is a shambles, and so unwritten? Think of the women in the show, so piercing and scary: look at Ruth (Julia Garner), the Ozark rat, with a clenched face and squeezed voice. She's uneducated, just feral, but feeling an alien urge to be respectable, and unable to utter the yearning that wants to be Mrs. Marty Byrde. Meanwhile the real occupier of that role, Wendy, accepts her ruined freedom and self-expression in becoming duplicitous and lethal. You guess she'll run for office in a future season; she is ready. I wonder about a hushed confrontation between that Wendy and Helen (Janet McTeer), the cartel lawyer, so refined, so groomed, so tall and implacable. One day perhaps the two of them may have a big scene together—but all Ozarkians should be fearful of seeing and hearing it.

We have twin sofas to watch from, Lucy and I; the binge is mutual; neither of us would think of watching without the other. Marty and Wendy keep saying they must tell each other everything; but then they turn secretive or isolated. And Lucy and I try to be decent, with about 0.01 percent of the money Marty has to launder. But one of the wicked lessons in *Ozark* is that laundering, discounting, lying to yourself and others comes with most money, no matter the amount. There is little protection or trust in the struggle to survive. The FBI man, Roy Petty, is the worst person in sight, but he loves his mother. Fatalism takes the place of humor, so Marty is a better parent to Ruth than to his own daughter.

Ozark is an open prison in which murder is not limited to people who get in your way. It is applied to vaguer things, like truth, law, society, and our future. Parts of Iceland are melting away; a similar dissolution is affecting the Statue of Liberty and the idea of a fair election. Meanwhile the Byrdes are reckoning to build a casino in Ozark, while urging their own kids to be honest and upright. The dark water of the lake can look calm in late light, but waterboarding is another current in the show.

Does that go too far? Well, the demon in *Ozark* lets us see how greed and calculation have smothered so many attributes or legends of our value. The option of murder, or removal—when you look away from the act and study your own press release—is becoming more reasonable or less exceptional. How else can the two of us list the murders, and wait for more? Why are so many shows now schedules of killing or breaking bad? *Ozark* (playing uninterrupted on Netflix) could be truer to itself with commercial breaks. The ads are a pulse that makes an engine in this modern Ozark. A red state can turn as ruby pretty as Dorothy's slippers. Wasn't she from Kansas?

Watching it together, making tea afterwards, still you can feel as alone as Marty or Ruth, staring into their close-ups with avid bewilderment. "Murder," the subject, can be a way of quietly acknowledging that so much in the world feels dead now, or dying, and we don't know whether to respond to that with grief. Or wrath. So must we settle for our oppressed solitude? Or do we think of some dark resort? Save the Union—or the archduke?

ALONE

Why alone? Or how?

There is something sad, yet secure, in this being alone. You may be on the Tube, halted between South Kensington and Gloucester Road reading this, or at 39,000 feet, crammed in a middle seat on a Dreamliner, but you can feel as isolated as Michael Corleone in his mansion, looking out at the lake, or as alone as his brother Fredo at one end of his fishing skiff.

I had written a first draft of this book, to be called *Murder at the Movies*, with a half-menacing, half cheery blurb—"a panorama of mayhem, a miscellany of malice." I was sitting in front of the screen and the text, and it was just me. You were a dream yet to come. Aren't reading and writing proofs of solitude as the human condition, and our wish to escape?

Then all at once "I Was Sitting There Alone" came into my head like a breeze. The window was open.

I won't say I fully understood this alternative title, but I felt it had a mythic clarity. Hopeful yet ominous, it was a shape in consciousness that contained the spectator or the reader settling into a murder mystery, the author planning how it would go, and the killer himself/herself, feeling the soft wind of an inviting but terrible notion.

For surely there is something unspeakable about this situation, murder. It seems to impose a moral isolation that is as frightening as it is seductive. But we are tempted by it, as if its forbidden nature is irresistible—as if we have always trusted (and dreaded) the irresistible to lead us on. And because its intrigue is something we have turned into a game, a whodunit? in which we can match the wit of a black knight offing the white queen. We are not sure how we do it, but we balance the dark intelligence in a killer with the sardonic omniscience of a storyteller who gets in bed with a murderer.

The killer, the teller, the audience—we make a warped triangle. This is how intelligence itself has a yearning to be bad or like an insurrection. It longs to think of something *new* and risky.

But real killers *are* appalling and the dead are to be pitied. And we . . . ? We watch the others as closely as spies, and then we look away.

Here in San Francisco, I have a short walk to the nearest post office, on Geary and Steiner. I get a sneaky thrill every time I go there, even if it is a place of tedium and travail. You see, this post office was built on the site of what had been the Peoples Temple, the ministry of Jim Jones, the place that sent "Jonestown" to Guyana in 1978.

That's not my only troubling thought as I walk to the mail. For I sometimes pass homeless people who have slept on the sidewalk. I know, this is San Francisco, a hallowed place of enlightened social policies. It is also a place where some residents cannot afford to live. So there is an overpass at Geary, and the homeless make a camp beneath it. They have ragged blankets, shopping carts, nervous pets, plastic bags of belongings, and the detritus of dire picnics. They seem aglow with fever or anger, or an illness that has smothered wrath.

They do not bear looking at, and I have noticed other passersby looking away as they head for the post office. I do try to examine these homeless faces and their sprawl in the sun, but without them noticing me. My sympathy stays detached and wary. I'm not sure I want to be involved. And they seem to have the same mixed feelings towards me. Side by side for a moment, we are alone.

These derelicts, these refugees from happy domesticity or American greatness, seem closer to death than the upright pilgrims going to the post. We calculate their future death, and may think about stopping to distribute a few scruffy dollars . . . until we decide that their plight is something the state, or the greater "we," should deal with. So we learn to walk with guarded gaze. And in our looking away we have managed to overlook how often "we" organize and preside over death. It's one of the quiet things societies do, like sending some to prison or bad schools or the unwholesome side of town. After all, so many of us will have to die—the bodies will need to be dealt with. That prospect leaves us tense, stricken, and dismayed, and so we want release—even a good murder story?

In that spirit, when the Peoples Temple building burned down some time after Jonestown, the city put up a post office. We do compartmentalize the wild spaces of the West. We try to keep a tidy set of boxes. In this book I examine those spaces—our room, our transformative screen on the wall, and the turmoil of the outer world it wants to organize and make acceptable. It is our dream that separation of the boxes will keep us safe, alive, and positive. But we are all of us sitting there alone, and wondering what will happen.

Jim Jones is now securely placed in a box labeled "destroyer . . . murderer." He deserves to be there, for in November 1978 it was Jones who ordered the killing of Congressman Leo Ryan, who was visiting Jonestown, the Temple's retreat in Guyana, to examine reports of bad stuff going down there and affecting his constituents (the 11th District, down the Peninsula from the city). The same day, 909 members of Jonestown died from cyanide poisoning, because Jim had persuaded them that they were under threat from hostile forces and even nuclear apocalypse. He told his people that this was the way for communists or socialists to die in an act of "revolutionary suicide."

It's easy to say the Jonestown box indicates insanity or something un-American and inhuman. But the truth is more complicated, and it involves our managing to walk past dying people on our streets. That was not Jim's way.

Born in rural Indiana in 1931, James Warren Jones was raised dirt-poor in a shack. He read intently and he was drawn equally to religion and to communism. He believed in salvation; he was outraged by the conditions in which so many unsaved people lived. By 1951, in the era of Joseph McCarthy, that was not an easy path. Nor was Jones helped by his heartfelt identification with people of color because of their poverty, their brave hopes, and their abiding outcast status. He was an evangelist, a racial integrationist, and a compelling speaker. He was a dark, handsome man who presented himself with a flourish. He opposed right-wing extremism and racism, and he was working to integrate Indianapolis. It sounds crazed. He and his wife adopted several children of color as well as having one child of their own. It was in 1956, still in the Midwest, that he founded the Peoples Temple.

He was a heroic figure then. His message of racism being defeated in the attack on poverty would win the support of Jerry Brown, Harvey Milk, George Moscone, Walter Mondale, and Willie Brown once he moved the Temple to northern California. Even then he had thought of taking the Temple away to a safer and more remote place, possibly in South America, because of intolerant opposition. Or because he felt an existential need to be alone. There were onlookers who began to detect ugly authoritarianism in Jones and the excessive fostering of his own cult. There were stories of him sexually abusing Temple members. He could seem intimidating, arrogant, and obsessed with his power. He did require his followers to donate their savings to the Temple, but few believed Jones was doing his work for money. He existed in a more wholly radical box in which the righteous may treat other people as figures in their drama.

In hindsight, it's easy to see that Jonestown had nowhere to go but disaster. But prophets of reform and doing good often live close to the peril of drastic solutions. It's not clear when Jim Jones thought of murder, or whether he ever saw it that way.

We can decide that Jones went mad—but he reckoned he was at work in a deranged society. Even in his act of mass murder, he believed he was saving his victims. He is the outstanding mass murderer in American history. He is "terrible" or "a monster." So can he be stricken from our record?

It didn't work that way; it seldom does with murderers. We cling to them and reenact their evil. The Jonestown story made for many books and documentary films. It was done as an epic: *Guyana Tragedy: The Jim Jones Story* (1980), a two-part television movie more than three hours long, directed by William A. Graham. Powers Boothe won an Emmy playing Jones in it. He was striking, and he strove to look like the real man. But whereas Jones's face was often a mask of harsh aloneness, actors deal in eloquence and communication. Casting Boothe, or anyone, was a sign of wanting to explain the killer, whereas it might be closer to the truth that Jones never understood himself. But he had wanted to be the central figure in some cataclysmic morality tale.

Perhaps he thought of his career as a movie. He said he was intent on helping others, but he became a ruinous celebrity. In our shocked culture, so few retain the names of his victims (nearly a third had been children; two-thirds were African-American).

The bodies were spread out in rows in the compound at Jonestown, without pain or individuality. Filmed murder is often like that. They had drunk the mix of grape Flavor Aid and poison and lain down together with blankets, the epitome of subservience. Far away in Guyana, they were like bodies at the end of our street, or in the places where the underclass goes to die. Jim Jones had become the director and the author of these people, and their self-imposed god. He took his own life at last, but he must have believed in his mastery. To murder someone, to administer death, you need to feel apart from the victim, like an author. It is an unnerving moral solitude jealous of the authority granted scripture's gods.

This aloneness is an endless ambiguity. We know we are locked in place by our unique consciousness; but we long to be "together" in love, in family, community . . . on the couch. We are told that loneliness is a danger, a dead end from which there may be no way back. But we also want to inhabit it, because it is the citadel of our selves, an ultimate independence. It is the vantage from which we judge and decide, and set ourselves up as creative and interpretive forces. So many writers come to the blank page feeling failures in life, but resolved to make another world in their words.

So many killers see life's circumstances as a stage they may control.

There's irony in that situation. The writer has to decide what to put on the blank page. That indecision can become a block, a nightmare, the futility of being a writer.

So maybe, alone in his room, impatient with his own lack of progress, trapped between *Once upon a Time* and The End, the writer decides to watch a movie and lets his empty screen flood with imagery, sequence, and apparent life. Oh, yes, that feels better. The congealed water has become a river.

Then the dream of power comes back. The writer can feel in charge of the flow. He could say, look, here is a character—rather attractive, definitely interesting, but unsettled. Hear what she says. See how she moves. Don't you wonder what she is thinking?

And then perhaps he'll kill her off. She could be Laura Hunt, or Diane Redfern (this is *Laura*, 1944). You can make up names and do some casting. Thus the story begins. The metaphor of creation is so appealing. Sitting here alone I could bring them all to life—and then polish them off.

You don't have to believe in God, or gods, but has it occurred to you that some creator has brought us to life with the unspoken assurance that we are all going to be offed?

No matter how grave and dreadful these murders are, don't rule out that chance of comedy. Stephen King complained that in filming his novel *The Shining*, Stanley Kubrick had abandoned its literary tragedy. He has a point, but that is just a prelude to seeing Stanley's *Shining* as one of the coldest comedies ever made, and an admission of how murder can get into our blood.

RED RUM

Here comes a candle to light you to bed,
And here comes a chopper to chop off your head!

Like children in a nursery rhyme, we warn ourselves about murder: don't do it, don't let it happen to you. But somehow the dire action becomes fit for play or dark jokes. In *The Shining*, RED RUM sounds like a pick-me-up for a cold winter's night—until we see that the scrawled word is in a mirror. The real thing says MURDER. That quirky inversion is a measure of how Stanley Kubrick—or the film's hotel—is in charge of these jittery characters. The story is going to be less about them than about that crooked triangle I spoke of: the characters, us, and authorship. It's a warning, but an encouragement, just like, "Attend the tale of Sweeney Todd!" at the start of that vibrant call to murder by Stephen Sondheim that sometimes has audiences giddy with laughter.

If you've not seen *Sweeney Todd* on stage, with the swirls of red silk when throats are cut, I assure you that its rendering of citizens into meat pies is an exhilarating trick, frightful but transporting. Sweeney is a fearsome protagonist who makes alienation lyrical. He runs a kind of concentration camp, yet Sondheim's soaring music and actors like Len Cariou and George Hearn have made Mr. Todd a hero for our desperate times. In the best productions you can taste his pies.

Is that shocking yet? Sooner or later in this book, we're going to have to wonder about what is called bad taste, and why it's hard to digest. The balance of elegance and nausea can be hard to sustain. You may wish to be somewhere else—until it occurs to you that this project could lead to a rousing medley of really terrific murders, some of the grisly scenes in history. (I know you have your favorites already.) Will we revisit classics like the shower scene from *Psycho*? Will there be alarming illustrations? Will we have the chance and the time to contemplate the adjacency of flesh and the point of a knife? Perhaps we should abandon illustration and let your imagination wonder? We don't want to run the risk of apparent exploitation. This has to be kept within the bounds of good taste.

I'm starting with *The Shining* (1980), the Stanley Kubrick adaptation of Stephen King, because of its pioneering balance of horror and satire, and its lethal-dainty script by Diane Johnson. So the Torrance family goes off to the Overlook Hotel in the bracing but desolate heights of Colorado. Life seems perfect there—everything the idiot mastermind Jack Torrance ever wanted. He will be caretaker for the off-season winter—time to write the novel he's always promised himself, time to defeat the blank pages. He can work alone in a vast room. His wife Wendy will go with him—she seems to have nothing else to do in life except be with a man to whom she is patently unsuited. Unless the point of their being at the Overlook is for Jack to despise her to a point of contemplating . . .

And Danny, their son, must go with them, too. Age six in the movie, he is an unusual boy: so intuitively smart or insightful—perhaps it's proper to hold him out of school for a winter, riding his plastic tricycle and Steadicam down the endless corridors of the Overlook, going from carpet to wood and back to carpet again. (The stylishness lets us know the hotel is haunted before ghosts gather.) Danny is needed there at the hotel because he shines, which means he can pick up on the secret foreboding in a place. This odd acumen has taught the boy to be afraid. Though Jack is supposed to be there to write a novel, it's Danny who half understands that the Overlook already has its story, a dormant fiction, full of dread, that may be awakened by careless caretakers.

Things go less than easily at the splendid hotel. Its story nags at the house, like the wind in the Rockies. The hotel is empty, but unnerving spirits linger with an odor of the past, or decay. They're trouble for the Torrances, but conspiratorial for us. We rather want the house to be haunted. Why else have we come to a horror film? Aren't we like Jack, daring the grisly tableaux of the hotel to frighten us?

Dad is acting strange and slipping back into his old depression; ghostly twin girls appear to Danny at the end of a corridor (like Alices in wonderland as seen by Diane Arbus); Jack finds a golden, empty bar, and when he closes his eyes and opens them again the gold has turned to liquor with a demon barman asking him, "What'll it be?" The Overlook refuses to be empty. We feel nervous about this, but we are helpless voyeurs at the hotel. In a kind of trance, Danny writes REDRUM on the wall and Wendy reads it in the mirror. Did Danny write this as himself, or is some presence using him to send a warning, in the form of a crossword clue? That's the odd charm of a film that mocks its own menace; and it's the unique sardonic tone of Stanley Kubrick. From the outset, we know, it's a picture about him, and about us waiting for blood and nastiness. The Overlook hints at horror yet does it as a tease.

Aha, you break in (please feel at home), looking to quell mounting disquiet—don't tell *us* we're preoccupied with murder, and don't run away with the idea that *anyone* believes murder is *ever* a game, or close to *fun*. Murder is very grave, you insist, and not at all pleasant.

You are correct, of course—murder is *not* at all pleasant, or anything to be encouraged; it should be banned. We don't teach it in school. It's horrid; it's bad; it's the last thing in the world you want to have come your way. In every Book of Best Behavior, all over the world, it's definitely proscribed as a no-no. Even the Nazis were against it.

I know what you feel you should say, and believe, about murder, and I respect you for it. But why do you watch so much of it if it is really hideous, or disturbing, or simply not your kind of thing? Do you realize that by the age of eighteen, the average American—I hope you aren't perturbed by being put in that gang—has seen 40,000 murders acted out?

Those 40,000 are killings we've seen depicted on screens. And the number can be more than 150,000 if you've survived to seventy. That's a lot of lives you've watched slip away. And you want to believe you are respectable, reliable? And safe? You wouldn't hurt a fly?

If you think of this in terms of Jack Torrance, and if you consider his life beyond the confines of his movie ... well, that's when you might weigh the rare saltiness of Jack Nicholson (our Jack Torrance), his depressed cunning, his sly mischief, his fraudulent normalcy, his smothered desire, and that way he walks. Walking in a movie is acting, of course, as much as talking or thinking; to stroll, to lurch, to hesitate, can be a mysterious, enchanting symbiosis of two Jacks, as one competes with the other. At the outset, some viewers felt that Nicholson was overacting: as if Jack Torrance should be real or ordinary. It's taken time to teach us that his posturing is that of someone who feels a ghost— the caretaker, Grady—wriggling into his soul and his drab clothes. Torrance has quiet fits all the time, especially when he's trying to be real and "agreeable."

Actors sometimes feel a character is taking them over, and that's not just creative wishful thinking, or a professional boast. It's something the audience wants to hear and imagine—like Daniel Day-Lewis making himself paralytic and speechless on the set of *My Left Foot* so that he had to be carried here and there in his wheelchair. And won his first Oscar for that brilliant helplessness!

Don't actors make this kind of sacrifice for us? Didn't Vivien Leigh take herself into actual mania while playing the deranged Blanche DuBois in *A Streetcar Named Desire*? Wasn't that commitment admirable—even if a doctor (or a husband) might have discouraged it? In fact, her husband, Laurence Olivier, actually directed her as Blanche on stage in London in 1949. Was that close to the situation of *Gaslight*, where a husband tries to suggest to his wife that she may be going mad?

The possibility of murder can whisper to the parties in settled marriages. It's like the delicate balance in watching a movie, and wondering what these enchanting yet risky people might do next. Jack Torrance from the start is a smothered charisma, the wry impulse of that relaxed but explosive Jack Nicholson, waiting to break out. From the first time I saw *The Shining* I felt uncomfortably at home with Jack. That clammy intimacy warned me to walk out on the film, to escape into the fresh air and the light. But I stayed.

Am I warning you about putting trust in an author, in me? Is that fair? Are you unsettled when I talk to you—as if you are really there? You have to realize that writers do imagine their readers: aren't they talking to us? Isn't it polite therefore if we *are* there, with some semblance of being attentive, or awake? Isn't that what engaged reading amounts to—the haunting of two solitudes?

Nor would the appeal of an empty Overlook be lost on any author. I enjoy deserts and an air of hollow authority—such as Jack Torrance might feel in his desolate place. And I have had a share of disappointment and depression—no need to grow morose with that confession. But authors crave solitude, *and* fame; they're quite or quietly mad—it's a good thing their creative energy is fixed on characters, and not real people.

Not that I would yield to violence, though I did once dislocate a young son's shoulder—it was an accident, one of those silly things, done in play, and a subject for enormous regret, and later teasing. It wasn't "interpersonal violence." Still, murder can occur suddenly and impulsively between people who are or have been in love. Which of us has lived long without feeling the surge of rage or despair growing out of disappointed affection and trapped commitment? It's natural, isn't it, as everyday as fuming, "Oh, I could kill you!" occasionally?

So when I saw one Jack as another, in 1980, I sighed as if to say, "Oh yes, I know this fellow—and I can tell this sinister film is going to turn out a comedy!" I recognized something I had been waiting for, a film enamored with the perilous irresponsibility that comes in watching films: that ultimate predicament— and thus, whatever the horror, it has to be ironic. Because pretending we're seeing the real thing, while sitting apart from it, is a wellspring of black humor. In the same way, Jack Torrance gets to the hotel and slowly intuits that the place knows him— he is home.

You aren't a murderer, are you? You don't have to answer that question, not even in your own privacy. I did try to Google how many people reading any particular book are likely to have committed a murder, but the celebrated system wasn't helpful.

That number is going to be so small it wouldn't really be useful, yet I suspect murderers do read books. They are inclined to be thoughtful, and detached. Murder often involves premeditation, and then the aftermath of that, which could be anything from remorse to delight, from guilt to exultation. Murder is one of those possibilities in life—like making love, or dying—over which most of us are going to ponder, night after night. And pondering is akin to reading (or writing). It is close to the devising of a storyline in which an author may realize, suddenly, "Oh, I see it now, I have to kill this character—just to move the story on." And that author is probably a cheery, good-natured soul, excited at breaking through a writer's block, even as he or she considers how to manage the death. It was Nabokov, with one eye on his mirror perhaps, who said, "You can always count on a murderer for a fancy prose style."

Warner Brothers tried to tell us in 1980 that *The Shining* was going to be a very frightening experience. What else could they have done? But the film is no such thing—not for viewers accustomed to that scary genre and its sudden swoops of fearful music. For all the persiflage of "You'll be too scared to stay at the Overlook," we longed to be there. It would be one thing in life to be alone in that echoing hotel with a wounded Jack Torrance coming after us, axe in hand. But on screen his maimed spider prowl slipped into wicked fun.

In fact, some hardcore horror enthusiasts were irritated that the scariness of *The Shining* wasn't quite delivered. Stephen King himself was disappointed. In advance, in trailers, we had seen those elevator doors with a slow waterfall of blood collapsing into view. But that highlight didn't really exist in the film, and big bad wolf Jack Torrance only actually murders one person—he puts the axe deep in Dick Hallorann (Scatman Crothers), who has come back to the Overlook to help the Torrance family. That is the only killing in the entire film! These days there'd be three or four dozen murders, done with a relish no one would have imagined possible in 1980.

So veterans like ourselves could be amused at the cheek of *The Shining* in pretending to be scary. You see, Jack is just an actor becoming a monster—that's what he tells himself. It's true, he can't write his novel; he's a bad husband and a questionable father; and still a hopeless dreamer—so we're talking ordinary American life.

The crucial scenes where Torrance meets Lloyd the barman (Joe Turkel) and Grady the waiter (Philip Stone) have a meticulous rapture as they dwell on the process of transference in all fictions. Those scenes are so tenderly written and so fondly acted that we revel in Jack being eased down his own dark hole. He's getting to be Jack, the Hyde who won't.

While we feel the threat to Danny, we don't worry that much over Wendy—I'm sorry, I have to say this: Shelley Duvall has had her moments on screen. But imagine if Wendy was Julia Roberts or Reese Witherspoon—braver women, more competent or sturdy. That becomes a different film in which we would feel bound to protect the threatened woman. But it's crucial in Kubrick, I fear, that Wendy seems pathetic or perfunctory. The director did consider a happy coda with Wendy and Danny safe in Denver, saying, "Phew!" But he dumped it to concentrate on Torrance.

Jack ends badly, if you want to see it that way: he doesn't write his novel; he has lost wife and son; he is frozen stiff in the maze. He's dead—but only for 1980. Much good that will do him at the Overlook, with its knack for bringing back the dead. By its code of existence, Jack has been drawn into the thrall of the great hotel built on a burial ground. He is the natural successor to Delbert Grady, the caretaker who ran amok in 1921 and murdered his own wife and child. So Jack is home and in his element—that's how the film closes on the exultant still photograph of him from July 4, 1921, another frozen moment. Happy birthday, everyone.

Wendy and Danny escape. But Kubrick wants them out of the way. It's Jack he's interested in, and now at last Jack is in a stealthy residence that is staring at us. A true sequel to *The Shining* could begin in an abandoned hotel, with some bright and eager family stopping at the door—they're lost, they took a wrong turning—and then the subtle anxiety and the withdrawn camera placement lets us realize Jack is watching them, and waiting. He is a ghost by now, or fully immersed in death—perhaps he whispers "Rosebud" to draw them in.

Alone with a blank page, the author needs just one word to set him off.

I COULD . . .

Really, you could. We all know the feeling and we might as well admit it. And don't take false comfort in its being a game. Just cross your fingers that you won't be put in the position of having to live with a concentration camp in the next village and pretending to be stupid. Those awkward neighborhoods can creep up on you.

The precious thing in a fiction is that our aspiring energy or suppressed hope may get some release at last. Jack Torrance doesn't really want a winter job, or a novel to his name. (It'll never be as successful as a Stephen King.) He wants his demon set free. You know that urge: if you own an automobile, you can't bear to think of it picking up a scratch, let alone a dent . . . or the hideous threat of a crash. But don't you love those movies where car after car is concertinaed and destroyed before bursting into rapturous fire? Cars get killed in movies as easily as people and give us a thrill of liberated damage.

I shouldn't say this. It could be too close to shouting "Fire!" in a packed theatre. We know how awful that would be: the panic, the rush, with some innocents trampled underfoot. And yet, fire can be exciting. I cannot forget that exhilarating moment in theatre, at the start of Shakespeare's *Henry V,* when the Chorus cries out, "Oh, for a muse of fire that would ascend the brightest heaven of invention . . ." We are dreamers, made that way, and photographed fire is so beautiful or ecstatic.

Movies came along at the moment when a soaring population (not just in numbers but in expansive hopes) began to knock against the obdurate facts of poverty, misery, disaster and . . . Our movies are a business; we sometimes like to call them works of art. But deeper down than those functions, they make a climate where impossible possibility is offered, where voyeurism is indulged and we are invited into pretty frames where space, light, happiness, and ease are mixed in with those pressing taboos, the orgy, *crash,* and murder. We can all get a look at those sensations for a trivial financial deposit—no commitment, no responsibility, just the imagining. Shoot! you say?

Some people undoubtedly fantasize about our current situation in which one *might* be forgiven for some wistful wondering over whether a malign and disastrous political leader should be . . .

And I daresay you recall His own wicked insight or boast about how, in a monster's grandeur and fame, *he* could go out on the street—and shoot anyone. He's dreaming all the time. Who else do you know so free from dull fact?

Once upon a time, in the dense forest of Germany, an un-named English gentleman, a sportsman, aimed his rifle at the begging figure of a great dictator, and . . .

In Geoffrey Household's adventure story *Rogue Male*, pub-lished in May 1939, his sportsman hero tells himself he is setting up to stalk the monster simply as a test of his hunting skills. Household never named the terrible target, though the sports-man who is captured before he can fire his gun, then tortured and nearly killed, will be hounded by unmistakably Gestapo forces in a desperate chase story. It's then the sportsman admits he would have fired—should have done so. After all, his fiancée had been murdered by the monster's thugs.

In 1939, as a magical sniper, would you have shot Hitler? You wouldn't hurt a fly? Or a rat? But 1939 was the last days of inno-cence. Suppose you bore the weight of extra knowledge that had accrued by 1945. Still, you might hesitate? Hesitation is the cusp of fantasy's pleasure. Perhaps you'd think back and weigh the consequences of those few shots fired in Sarajevo in June 1914 by the muddled, inept Gavrilo Princip when the archduke's car took a wrong turning. One shot can kill so many. A part of us still thinks of warning that feeble archduke.

By 1941, Fritz Lang, who had himself quit Germany in 1933, made a film in Hollywood, *Man Hunt*, taken from the House-hold novel. Walter Pidgeon played the sportsman. Joan Bennett is the London tart who helps him. It's well done in a 1930s way that still alarmed the Hays Office for being anti-German. It's not as compelling as the remake, *Rogue Male*, from 1976, directed by

Clive Donner, adapted for the screen by Frederic Raphael, with Peter O'Toole as the sportsman. O'Toole brought a passion to the hunter's mission. Seven when war broke out, he had grown up hating Adolf, obsessing over him and knowing he was evil. He often said *Rogue Male* was the favorite of his pictures.

There's talk of another *Rogue Male* remake now, with Benedict Cumberbatch as the hero. I doubt the story will stop there. The hesitant assassin is a figure lodged in our mythology, the armed man (or woman) who says, "I could . . ." If we're going to have heroes and villains, there comes a moment when our good guy may feel the dark necessity of eliminating the monster. The American action film where heroism is put to the test has always been a shooting gallery. But the trick is for the shootist to understand a Hitler before history has had time to reach its verdict.

Here's the delicate point: it's hard in a movie to have a character pick up a gun, take careful aim . . . and not have him fire it. There's a pregnant, waiting permission in the structure of the medium that whispers, "Fire me." They shoot films, don't they?

It's possible to fall for the storylines of narrative cinema, the show business trick, to believe that good will triumph, along with true love and the happiness we deserve. But beneath those homilies there is a lurking pressure, the unhealed suggestion that we are poised at the other end of the voyeur line, ready to open fire. How can it be that generations of directors and cinephiles stay pledged to the theory that film is not an inducement to violence?

IT'S NOT FAIR

But it's not quite fair. It never was.

The routine of creation or giving birth is known as sweet and positive; it all seems in order—as if some benevolent force had presided over it. In a similar way, the life on screen flows before us. It does not require our consent or our labor. Its momentum is fatalistic or irresponsible: if this flow keeps on going on, we're going to grow older . . . do we have to die?—yet we seem so alive. All motion pictures ask of us is to sit there and revel in the shifts of light and watery motion.

But Sweeney Todd knows,

> There's a hole in the world.
> Like a great black pit
> And the vermin of the world
> Inhabit it

Sweeney says the hole is London—but it could be anywhere because we know somehow at the movies that that passing river is not entirely benign. Who knows if at dusk, an arm may not reach out of the water, like the dreamed salute of a corpse in *Deliverance*, that scary story of disaster lurking in the wonders of the northern Georgia wilderness and a seething river. You know you're going to have fun at the movies—but do be careful, and ask yourself whether you shouldn't leave *now*, while there's time.

You feel this is alarmist? Well, alarm can be a siren song we can't resist. Once upon a time, off the friendly Massachusetts shore, a pretty girl went skinny-dipping at night in the warm Atlantic. You saw her body rolling in the blue sea, as if she was a fish. You didn't know her, but she seemed like a good girl. From deep below you saw her fluttering on the surface of the water. Then there was music in the sea, some darker presence. If it was another fish, it seemed to be approaching. With intent. Just as you can't have a gun in a movie without it being fired, so pretty girls may have to be set off, too.

Did you guess the ominous approach would carve her apart—absolutely frightful to think about—yet you wanted it? There was really no future in *Jaws* if that opening scene didn't provide the enterprise with a good-looking corpse. We have so many movies, even on dry land, where a pretty girl is going to turn up dead to start a story. Can you imagine your own sweetheart being ripped and shredded by such teeth? Can you contemplate the damage? Yet you wanted such an outrage to trigger the action?

I can believe you've watched every television story from *Law & Order* (456 episodes) and become a forensic connoisseur at the discovery of so many corpses in alleys, parking lots, trash bins, and even their own beds. But may I say your being so eager is not entirely nice.

The invitation of the screen has always been barbed or compromised. We love life, but we gather there to contemplate death.

We didn't ask to be born—is that why we weep at the initial moment, coming into the hole in the world? Long before we realize the inescapable narrative line that has been set up for us! For being born means we're going to have to die. There's no escape from it, no alternative. Do you see how murder can be a gesture to defy this merciless unfairness imposed on us? Do you begin to understand your anger?

This matter of unfairness is structural. You simply woke up, or came to, in this impossible place, and people told you it was Eden? So smile?

You don't need a lawyer to make your plaintiff case. There you are, Cain, the first citizen born on Earth. So you till the earth (it's closer to fresh air and exercise than trying a novel) while your kid brother Abel keeps the sheep and seems a fine guy. Then one day, you offer your work—fruit and vegetables—to the Lord, all organic stuff. While Abel gives him lambs. You could imagine a fair and impartial Lord putting those things together and having everyone over for Sunday dinner, rack of lamb with potatoes, green beans, chard, and yams. With peaches and grapes for dessert.

But No! That Lord of ours had respect for Abel's gifts, "But unto Cain and his offering he had not respect."

Ladies and gentlemen of the jury, was that fair?

There's not a trace of incriminating backstory in Genesis. No justification. There's no hint that Cain was lazy in the fields, that he sometimes maimed a passing rabbit, or thought lewd thoughts about Eve, his mother. He didn't sit under a tree writing bad poetry, or plotting the downfall of the kingdom, like a communist. All he did was work his butt off in the sun to make the best vegetables any Lord or Alice Waters could ask for. Was he created just to demonstrate the narrative function of murder?

So he's blamed for killing Abel—and wasn't that part of God's unkind scenario? The revenge is acted out in a classic version of this story, Elia Kazan's *East of Eden* (1955), taken from the Steinbeck novel. That doesn't seem to be a murder movie, yet see how it gets rid of an awkward character. Removal can be murder.

In idyllic peaceful Salinas, California, in 1916, Adam is a farmer with two sons, Aron and Cal. Aron is a bright boy, a high school football captain, with a wide brow and ardent eyes, as played by Dick Davalos. He has this sweet girl Abra (Julie Harris), and he will marry her one day, so his father Adam (Raymond Massey) smiles on them and the wonder of such a son.

Dick Davalos really was a good-looking guy—but he didn't have a chance. For his director, Kazan, that dark, vengeful, brilliant betrayer of established virtues, was turning the fable upside down. He had found this brooding wild child actor, James Dean, to be his Cal. And in his smothered wrath at unfairness, Dean was a new god for 1955—he seized the world's rebel imagination. So Cal yearns for Adam's respect as much as he wants Abra for himself, and he is hurt at being overlooked. He gives Adam money, money he's earned growing beans, and all Aron offers for Adam's birthday is a smile and the announcement that he and Abra will be married. So Adam prefers Aron.

Whereupon, Cal sinks into darkness and revenge. He takes Aron to Monterey to meet their wicked mother (Jo Van Fleet), who runs a whorehouse in that racy town and surveys the world with contempt. That mother once tried to kill Adam. This revelation is more than Aron can endure. There is no need to murder Aron. The bright boy is so shocked by his mother that he runs away and enlists in the Great War. He removes himself. So Cal is left in Salinas to care for Adam, who has had a stroke from the stress. And Cal has Abra with him, like a bride. He has respect and ownership at last. He might write a novel.

Cal did not need to rise up and slay Abel in the fields—one glance was enough, with the knowledge it carried. We still speak of killing glances and practice them in the shade beneath the tree of knowledge. Michael Corleone (Al Pacino) needs only to look at his helpless brother Fredo, and then pass that look on to Al Neri, his patient executioner. We love Fredo (John Cazale, when it was apparent the actor was dying), but we know he has to go. The look on Michael's dead face is as compelling as the medium.

And if life is a brotherhood, even for only children, we understand that one brother strives to surpass another. The brothers Karamazov are caught up in that dynamic; it is what sustains their unease. Raskolnikov in *Crime and Punishment* (1866) kills out of his extreme poverty—that explanation is available for any realist critique. But he is driven by a deeper urge, a revenge, in response to his unasked-for life and the existential horror of being born without any power over himself. Murder is an idea that popularly succumbs to material motivation—the suspect did it for money, for power, to avoid boredom, or because he was angry at seeing a dog turd on his shoe? But murder can be a purer thing, an *acte gratuit*, and on the movie screen it can come to us like our virgin, a miracle, or the shark that we dreamed up. The screen and the light have always guessed that we nurse thoughts of murder in our dark, and the gift or assurance in movies is how things can appear unbidden, out of a deep subconscious.

The intimacy of the movies and their night-light is the way a murder can be indulged, without pain or damage, let alone capture and punishment. But the cinema is a fearful demon. It knows its vast power of persuasiveness or suggestion—it knows it can say, look, there is the naked woman, have your way with her—she'll never know she's in your dream. Or it can say, look, there is the knife—it can be your knife—or would you prefer a chainsaw or a modest nuclear weapon? Is it coincidence that the culture that made the movies has also furnished itself with an armory of weapons that would be hilarious or ridiculous if the armed state weren't so intimidating?

The offer is there and it makes for the business's money and our dreaming. But offering us these dreamy delights is such a gamble. We might turn into real rapists and murderers, so the profession of cinema has always talked about codes, safeguards, and censorship, declared that it would not let the liberty of such ideas and prospects go without rebuke. Every killer was to be caught and punished. So let him go on a killing spree for eighty-five minutes—and then have "justice" reign in the last five?

Unless he was Gavin Elster, the killer in *Vertigo*, getting away with it all. That's not fair, unless you are willing to give special license to the authority and beauty that directors like Alfred Hitchcock can command when it comes to murder.

Ostensibly, *Vertigo* concerns a detective, Scotty Ferguson (James Stewart), hired to watch over the disturbed state of Gavin's wife, Madeleine (Kim Novak). She thinks she may be someone else, so she wanders around San Francisco, seemingly unaware that Scotty—and we—are trailing her. But the private eye is really a stooge, and we are suckers, too. Madeleine *is* someone else, and the plot is conceived as a murder story by Gavin, no matter that he appears in only a few sequences. He wants his wife dead (it seems to be for money, but it could be out of boredom, too). So he has enlisted another woman, Judy (Novak, of course), to pose as his wife. She will take Scotty in a seductive process of hushed pursuit until she leads him up a fatal tower.

You see, Gavin knows Scotty can't handle heights because the detective suffers from vertigo. So Gavin will be at the top of the tower with the dead Madeleine (Gavin has offed her, never mind how, or ask how he carried her dead weight up all those steps), and then he'll throw her off the ledge. Vertigo—bingo. She will be regarded as a suicide. After the crime, Scotty is a wreck. Judy can get lost. Gavin is in the clear. This absurd plot is a measure of our willingness to be deceived by the gravitational pull of murder. The longer we gaze upon Kim Novak in the film, the more certain it is that she must die—whoever she is. Forget suicide, or Gavin's wicked design; it's voyeurism that oppresses her.

Gavin's motive is immaterial. His presence is theoretical (only a little more substantial than the cameo appearance of Hitchcock, his fellow in misdirection). The real subject is Scotty's mortification. And so, finally, Gavin is never detected, captured, and executed, though he has two deaths on his hands. Hitchcock had reckoned the censorship code would insist on Elster being punished. He actually filmed a small sequence where it is reported that the wicked Gavin has been captured and charged. Then Hitch dropped that scene—and no one noticed or complained.

Vertigo seems to be real and San Francisco. The mood of dream only seeps in slowly, leaving the actual city like an attractive somnambulist. Elio Petri's *Investigation of a Citizen Above Suspicion* (1970) is more surreal and diagrammatic. An Italian police inspector (Gian Maria Volonté) murders his mistress (Florinda Balkan—she is then allowed flashbacks where she rehearses her own death). How will you do it this time? she asks him seductively. He cuts her throat while making love to her. Quick and not too bloody—it's the idea of cancellation more than slaughter. She still looks pretty.

There seems to be no more motive than wanting something to do—or devising a test of the police system. He is a recently promoted inspector, zealous, fierce, and fascistic. Indeed, Volonté plays him as rather a bore, monotonously obsessed with his kindergarten Kafka act in which crime and inquiry dance a tango. He contrives to become leader of the investigation into the mistress's death. He builds evidence against innocent suspects, but then he says oh, no, it can't be them. At which point he establishes a case against himself. It seems solid. He confesses, only to be told, no, it can't be you. He is above suspicion. This is a mock thriller, a farce about police authority, and the calm admission that murder is so pure a passion it hardly needs motive or character.

Investigation won the Oscar for Best Foreign Picture, but it has dated in ways that leave exposed the satirical structure of inversion. I think Lubitsch could have made a masterpiece out of it—with Cary Grant as the man? (There was a plan for a remake. Paul Schrader wrote a script. Al Pacino was thinking of playing the inspector. Who would you like as the mistress? Sometimes unmade projects are more enticing than a movie wrapped and delivered.)

But inversion lingers like a scent over murder stories. Patricia Highsmith's *The Talented Mr. Ripley* was published in 1955. Her character, Tom Ripley, feels an urge to murder for its own sake. Set aside the leverage of money, power, or advantage; you can even retire any thought of revenge. There might be a murder done almost by chance, like skimming flat stones on a lake. There is no other motive in Tom's busy mind. He sees the task of killing his new chum, a perfect, arrogant shit named Dickie Greenleaf, as a puzzle. Until he reaches this fulfilling insight:

> He had just thought of something brilliant; he could become Dickie Greenleaf himself. He could do everything that Dickie did. He could go back to Mongibello first and collect Dickie's things, tell Marge any damned story, set up an apartment in Rome or Paris, receive Dickie's cheque every month and forge Dickie's signature on it. He could step right into Dickie's shoes.

Tom could become an actor playing a part—and wasn't that more appealing than being his own drab self?

There have been films of the Highsmith novel—*Plein Soleil* (1960), by René Clément, with the iconic displaced Alain Delon in the lead, or *The Talented Mr. Ripley* (1999), by Anthony Minghella, with Matt Damon as a poor, lonely boy working his way towards being gay. But a pure nihilist malice shines out of the situation of these films, a kind of revenge against having life: perhaps Tom does it in existential irony, as an exercise or a hobby, to pass the time, and as a response to the absolute unfairness in being alive. Who knows whether cinema will ever get all the way to that nihilism? Perhaps we'll have to be a little less than humane to handle that coldness. But maybe we're getting there? The cinema could deliver that cultural future in which we give up reality and responsibility for imagining. And murder is one of our abiding dreams, for it gives life to that undeniable instinct that, truly, other people are not quite as good as us. They hardly deserve us. It's not fair. But we're alone. Sitting there watching.

And not nice, you hasten to add. A feeling of disquiet is growing in you again that, really, this curious half-comic treatment of murder is too upsetting. It shouldn't be a topic for mirth, should it? Unless mirth is the last way left to awaken us to the pain and the loss.

We have earlier, classic examples of that shock effect. In 1729, Jonathan Swift put out a pamphlet, "A Modest Proposal for preventing the Children of Poor People From Being a Burthen to Their Parents or Country, and For Making them Beneficial to the Publick." The thrust of the essay was to say, look, in Ireland the poor are suffering terribly and they have little in the way of assets except their own children, who are so close to starving. What logical recourse is there but that the children, the babes, be sold to the rich as delicacies and choice food stuffs: "A young healthy child well nursed, is, at a year old, a most delicious nourishing and wholesome food, whether stewed, roasted, baked, or boiled; and I make no doubt that it will equally serve in a fricassee, or a ragout."

Swift more or less accommodated the rattled public explanation that he had written the Modest Proposal in a vein of satire, or comfortable fun—as an artful way of drawing attention to "a problem." But that veil of politeness only half obscures the economic logic of what he was saying. Ireland in the 1720s is a long way away now; it easily seems quaint, or *sui generis*. Until you think of the derelicts on the streets of San Francisco, and the accommodation we make with ourselves to pass their tableau by.

So let us be more pointed by suggesting that in America in 2019 there are wealthy people paying scant taxes on exorbitant incomes so that the increasing number of "the poor" have to support these rich people in their state of well-being. This seems ridiculous or out of order, but it is so. In not so indirect a way, this leads to the premature deaths of some of the poor people. They cannot eat, so before they become nothing but impossibly chewy bone and withered skin let's factory farm them and serve them up as plump chicken tenders. At a level of actual yet surreal understanding, they may feed the wealthy—and be useful. You can call that madness, or you can admit its insight into what is happening. Every day we are murdering and consuming our own people. Sweeney's famous meat pies are not just a theatrical conceit.

Cannibalism masked in cuisine is not out of our question. Think of how we need to eat, in a world where food has run short or been compromised. Over events like the siege of Leningrad, we are still discreet about what was eaten. In Cormac McCarthy's novel *The Road* (2006), the devastated landscape discovers such things as a baby being roasted on a spit. At such times, having fire and cuisine may overwhelm questions of taste.

Nearly a hundred years after Swift, in 1827 in London, Thomas De Quincey wrote another essay, "Murder Considered as one of the Fine Arts." He extolled murder as a theatre for human ingenuity, grace, and self-expression—like music or wit and all the other staples of our imaginative being?

De Quincey imagines a fictional Society for the Encouragement of Murder, and then plunges into its formal and demented proceedings in a lampoon of academic process (and the way that bureaucracy can obscure cruelty):

> Now, if merely to be present at a murder fastens in a man the character of an accomplice; if barely to be a spectator involves us in one common guilt with the perpetrator; it follows of necessity, that, in these murders of the amphitheatre, the hand which inflicts the fatal blow is not more deeply imbrued in blood than his who sits and looks on: neither can he be clear of blood who has countenanced its shedding; nor that man seem other than a participator in murder who gives his applause to the murderer, and calls for prizes in his behalf.

Once again, the panic defense was mounted that De Quincey was no worse than a heartless but delicious satirist, as opposed to a writer who had found a fresh insight on awkward truth. The only creature he had ever killed, he said, was a plundering tomcat in his pantry. He stressed the incredible: that in polite, literate society (this was seventy years in advance of the movies) the allegedly disastrous and unkind act of murder had been turned into an entertainment or an art, and above all a business in which the public—those good souls—were effectively digesting the corpses created by lifelike murders. This is more than a joke or a flourish of wit. It is a direct accounting of the ways in which we regard murder as a true response to the unfairness of life.

Isn't it a black mark on academe that one can't major in murder at Oxford or Harvard when so many students give hours a day to watching it? Where is the grant-in-aid that our preoccupation deserves? And if the Nobel people feel confident about awarding a prize for peace (which can be a very ambivalent pursuit), I wonder whether they might not notice the purity, the passion, and the dedicated craft that can attend murder.

If by any means there was a campaign of protest and censorship—on the principle that it is so wicked—so that depictions of murder would be banned from our showtime, there would be outrage, rioting on the streets, et cetera. There are those of us who would defend murder to the death.

WHAT IS AN OVERLOOK?

"Well, it's a vantage, with an advantage," said Lucy.

You know this setup. You were introduced to it, I suppose, by Hannibal Lecter in *The Silence of the Lambs* (1991), in a high-tech isolation cell at the end of a dungeon corridor. That's where Clarice Starling had to seek him out, as he sat in tethered splendor, as groomed as prison garb allowed, but as still and saturnine as a Great Actor could be on his way to an Oscar for just twenty minutes of screen time. Authority oozed out of him, like a mix of eau de cologne and formalin.

We knew how bad Lecter was: we got the rhyme with "cannibal" and we heard the reference to his being a reader even if we were unsure of the etymology. But this Lecter's imprisonment had led to a kind of enthroned solitude, a dispassionate hotel room that only fostered his cult of intelligence. He could work so much out from there. He could be in charge. He was a monster, but adorable. A weird religious respect was in the air. And Anthony Hopkins smiled to himself and did cunnilingus on words like "chianti" or "Clarice." What a role it was! What authorship it contained.

If it suited you, you could say Lecter was "mad," but what help is that? Smarter than anyone around, he might have been humming "Psycho Killer, qu'est-ce que c'est?" that Talking Heads song from 1977, with David Byrne wailing out the "Yeah yeah yeah yeah!"

That song is used in the second episode of *Mindhunter*, the Netflix series created by Joe Penhall in which a nerdy FBI man, Holden Ford, develops a hobby of talking to serial killers. He seeks them out in their I-was-sitting-there-alone places, and tries to engage them in his half-baked innocent way. He goes to Vacaville State Prison in California to interview Ed Kemper, a six-foot-nine little boy with a Hitler mustache and a six-foot-ten I.Q. He's a serial killer—very nasty. But he's so much more informed than Holden that he makes the FBI man seem suspect or insecure. You cannot watch *Mindhunter* without beginning to feel that the investigator harbors some longing to be a serial killer too.

"You see, that's what binge-watching is," said Lucy. "It's one damn killer after another."

I should have guessed: the episode we were watching was directed by David Fincher. Remember that name.

The Overlook in *The Shining* seems like a swank resort hotel in the wilderness (it was modeled on the Ahwahnee in Yosemite and the Timberline Lodge beneath Mount Hood in Oregon). That makes it as beautiful and as enigmatic as . . . a large, well-appointed but empty theatre, waiting for an audience and a movie. I realize such venues are becoming as antique as Roman theatres, but if you've ever known such a vacant heaven—one with 2,000 seats, or more—then you may appreciate its enchanted air, the mix of spatial splendor and secret (or as yet unrevealed) promise. An empty theatre is like Creation without the juice of purpose or desire. At the Overlook, you'll have the best view but you will be "over" it, above it. You'll be able to watch and imagine without having to intervene or feel culpable.

The name of the place ought to help us feel a metaphor for a movie house, a place where our spectatorship is never in jeopardy. The *Titanic* may sink, but we'll stay dry. Whereas a real Overlook Hotel would survey range upon range of Rockies— the magnificence of nature, and a world into which you could ride, hike or fly—the movie theatre Overlook has an extra, vital security. If there are bears and mountain lions in the Colorado silence (or even escaped convicts), they can come up to the glass (as it were); they can look at where we are; but they can't get in at us and put us to the test of their claws or their teeth. Can they?

There's a Ray Bradbury story, "The Veldt." It appeared in 1950—so prescient. The Hadley family lives in the future in a HappyLife Home that is all automated. The kids, Peter and Wendy, have a room with screens for walls. They could program it to any scene. But they insist on the veldt, with lions prowling in the middistance. This so unnerves the parents that they plan to disable the screen. But Peter and Wendy trap them in the room and next day, somehow, those high-minded parents are found dead. It looks as if they have been mauled by lions. The analogy in that story never loses its grip.

Movie was not just a clever extension of theatre, with rows of spectators attending to a performance, breathing the same air as the actors and staying quiet to hear what they had to say. That old model included the potential in which a member of the audience might leap up on the stage and intervene: that happened at Ford's Theatre in Washington on April 14, 1865, and it still occurs when heartfelt cheers from an audience put a blush on an actress's face. That affection doesn't grace or warm the movies, where the players don't know the spectators exist. And where the audience doesn't care that the players may be deceased. Their not being there is a kind of death, and it was observed by Norman Mailer how far the entire enterprise of movie is a reminder of death.

From the outset, the movies dealt in impossibility. They showed us things we could not see in actuality—like the bright green Wicklow meadows standing in for drab, muddy Agincourt in Olivier's *Henry V*, or, in 1899, glimpses of the Egyptian pyramids, the jungles of Sumatra, or the look on Tolstoy's face and the way he walked. They also foresaw the chance of making visible things that could not be: so Georges Méliès conceived a trip to the Moon seventy years or so before Stanley Kubrick conjured up the deep space of *2001*. But those miracles were minor or polite marvels compared with cinema's urge to show us things we *should* not see.

The commercial momentum of filmgoing identified its natural thematic material: situations of danger or suspense that did not actually threaten audiences; windows of sexual allure that did not immediately take spectators (mostly male) into the divorce courts; and tests of epic violence in which law-abiding cowards in the dark could feel they had fought for virtue and justice. But as the business became a sensation there were warnings from respectable society about the indecent stress on fantasy in what was called cinema. Dreaming seemed a natural human activity; it might repay interpretation; but could it undermine the wholesome working of a new mass society? Did "realism" still have a moral point? The history of censorship reflected that urge for guardianship, but the safeguarding codes would also permit the movies to depict the falling veils of nakedness and the steps towards murder without theatres being closed down. You can call this demoralization, or you can see it as the tricky playfulness that movies ushered in. Censorship has always been a subgenre in movies—and nowadays almost the only films I *have* to see are those I cannot see. Or so I thought until the dismaying *The Other Side of the Wind* was finally given a mortician's rouge.

In every instant, good cinema is saying, no, you can't see this, you really shouldn't. Take a moment from *The Shining* that demonstrates this principle. Jack Torrance goes to room 237 at the Overlook. His son, Danny, has stopped at that room already, but it was locked. It had the taut air of a forbidden place. As Jack goes there, the film is intercut with shots of the visionary Danny trying to resist what his Dad may find. But the doors to 237 are open now, and a first-person camera tracks in (the entry is so fluent). We see Jack's hand pushing against the bathroom door that is tactfully ajar.

He enters and beholds a bath with its plastic curtain half drawn. The bath is empty. But then we have a shot of Jack—head on—staring at it, as if summoning some spirit. We cut back to the bath and there is now a visible body, sitting behind the curtain. Its hand reaches out and draws the plastic sheet aside; we see a female form. Jack smiles in wonder. The woman slowly stands. She is tall, slender, Nordic-looking, naked, with wet hair (the actress was Lia Beldam—she said later that Nicholson was "absolutely charming" and treated her with "great courtesy"). She gets out of the bath, fully frontal; we see breasts and her pubic hair. She is being made available by the Overlook for Torrance, but she is on offer to us too, to gaze at and conjure.

She takes Jack in a wordless embrace—can't we imagine ourselves in her warm, wet arms?—and they kiss. Jack is in shut-eye rapture until something seems amiss. He is in a close-up with just the rim of her head in which one eye seems to exist in a cave instead of the full roundness of a young face. Then Jack feels horror as he looks over her shoulder at a mirror—another screen—and sees that she is old with flabby flesh, mottling, scars. She is so entirely unfresh, a freakish old woman. She starts to laugh at him. "Beauty" has switched to decay. His lust has turned to paranoia—and what has happened to us?

This scene would require an R rating (the woman's body is still blurred in some TV screenings), but it is nearly forty years old and chaste next to what we're accustomed to now. The sequence taunts offering and what you might call room service in a hotel like the Overlook—or in Las Vegas or other places where a naked woman might be served with a plate of garnished smoked salmon and a nice Sancerre. The enterprise of the cinema is being put on a par with a resort hotel—our movies have always been close to television commercials for corrupt luxury. They are serving up the meat for our fantasies—and in that process they are licensing and indulging taboos against ravishing or murder. The beauty in the bath is suddenly a portent of death. In embracing Jack she is foreplay to his grave. That is the horror he feels.

But a faux nude in your bath is going only so far. Let's take another offering, closer to the core of this book, an opportunity for murder dropped in our innocent lap. I use that word because in the normal way of things going to a movie is one of those situations that does provide the human being with a lap. Moreover, that curious yet pleasing human function disappears when we stand up. Is there any other part of the body with that trick?

Two men bump into each other on a train: one is an alleged tennis star looking like Farley Granger—not just handsome but pretty, though slightly weak. His name is Guy Haines. The other man is Bruno Anthony—fancily dressed in co-respondent shoes with his name embroidered on his tie, and as insinuating as Robert Walker could make him. For a decade, Walker had tried to be a boyish lead actor in pictures, but that path had failed him. He was too troubled; some acid began to curdle his sweetness. Alfred Hitchcock grasped this change. Walker would be dead a couple of months after the film opened, in a mix-up of drugs, booze, and fatalism. But here he is, an ingratiating villain or a decadent hero—so much more interesting than his new acquaintance. Guy has a big athletic career while Bruno does nothing except ride the train. Guy is active, Bruno is passive, but he drives the picture.

Bruno is drawn to Guy (there is a swoon of gay admiration), and Guy is amused by this unpredictable stranger. But Bruno gets very serious when sharing one of his ideas.

He understands that in the best tactful way some of us would not mind if someone we knew was dead, or out of the way. For example, Bruno has a loathed father, and Guy has this awkward and rather vindictive wife, Miriam, back in Metcalf in Connecticut. Don't ask how Guy and Miriam ever got together when they seem so hostile—perhaps they were desperate for sex in a foolish half hour. But they are separated now and Guy wants to marry Ann Morton, the daughter of a senator and as lovely and dull as Ruth Roman can manage. Ann offers a rewarding way ahead for a tennis player once he's stowed his racket. But Miriam is being difficult about a divorce.

Bruno's idea is simple and piercing. Why don't he and Guy

swap murders? There's no hint in this proposal that the killings would be immoral. The essential in murdering someone is not being found out, or feeling responsibility—having the mess in your lap. But suppose I murder your wife and you take care of my father. We can do the jobs in a professional spirit, without undue emotional involvement. No one is going to associate us with the murder of people we never knew. It's a sly allusion to the way we can watch a movie killing—observe it being planned and executed, sitting there alone—without taking the blame. Or feeling guilty.

Guy is not smart. He regards Bruno as just an idle joker. He doesn't have our eyes for appreciating Robert Walker, and of course he doesn't know he's in a movie where something *has* to happen. Plot is a hurricane that is always coming. Guy seems potent in society, but Bruno the hapless outsider runs the picture.

This film is Alfred Hitchcock's *Strangers on a Train* (1951), scripted by Raymond Chandler and Czenzi Ormonde, with assists from Whitfield Cook and Ben Hecht, but rooted in the 1950 novel by Patricia Highsmith, that disconcerting genius in matters of murder. Guy is not a tennis player but an architect in the book, but the story grasps the thrill in the swapped murders and the way that theory calms the outrage. And surely Hitchcock was as aware as Kubrick of how easily this transaction mirrored the situation of being at the movies, seeing something we shouldn't be seeing.

This climaxes in what you'd have to call the successful killing of Miriam. As played by Laura Elliott, in spectacles, Miriam is more spiteful than pretty. Hitch gives us no reason to feel any sympathy for her. She doesn't have Guy's baby, or even a dog. Whereas it would be possible to redraw the story and have Miriam as a likable small-town wife who has been dumped by an ambitious social-climbing bastard of a husband. She could be appealing and in love with Guy, still, in her hopeless way. The baby or the puppy could become endearing. Think of Jane Wyman as that Miriam.

Instead, when Bruno finds Miriam at twilight in a fairground in Metcalf, she is with another man. But once she thinks the classier Bruno is interested in her she's ready to abandon this chump. In her grasping way she flirts with Bruno so we can decide she deserves to be punished.

As the sequence builds, we are "with" the rogue Bruno in an overlook of complicity. We know what he intends; we feel his purpose tending against Miriam and her petty selfishness. When Bruno pops a child's balloon with his cigar we chuckle at his meanness. As he follows Miriam we are following too. Don't be offended, but you have never strangled a bad girl, have you? Then how are you such a willing aide to what is going to happen here? Is it the intellectual satisfaction of Bruno's plan that appeals, or is the whole process reaching into some forbidden urge in you without blood, unpleasantness or losing one's breath?

The amusement park has a tunnel of love, a lake with little boats and a "magic isle." That's where Bruno follows Miriam. He detaches her from her local beau and then he moves on her very swiftly. He wraps his gloved hands around her throat. He had complained to Guy that he never did anything, but now he has become a bold killer who makes Guy's tennis seem fatuous. Miriam's eyes bulge, she struggles and her spectacles fall off. Nothing is accidental in Hitchcock. On the ground, those glasses provide a refracting lens through which he can show us the lethal act. It is languorous; it is swollen; it is baroque. And in the warping optics we see the figure of Bruno throttle the woman and then lower her to the ground and into the lens, offering the corpse *to our laps* in the way a retriever might bring us the warm body of a duck just shot. She is a gift to us and we have earned it.

The ethics are tidied up at the film's close. Bruno perishes. The supposed suspense is settled. Guy and Ann can be together— until tedium prevails. In retrospect it's easy to conclude that *Strangers on a Train*, a grand success in its day (enough to rally Hitch's faltering reputation), is a silly film, not just implausible but unnecessary (the worst fate for old movies), except in one respect. The device of the exchanged murders looms in the air like a lever waiting to be gripped. Walker's Bruno is an unnerving character, smart yet disturbed. And the murder of Miriam is among the most absorbing set pieces in Hitchcock. We can call that good direction and adroit writing. We may give credit to the cinematographer, Robert Burks. But the secret to the scene is its understanding of something so embedded but perverse that censorship never noticed it. A murder can be the best thing in a picture: it's the privileged view from an Overlook. For Hitchcock, it was the point of making movies, and thus it tries to hide his fear of life and ordinary death.

A NICE ENGLISH MURDER

Hitchcock was English, till the end. Even when he got on an American highway, driving up to Fairvale in northern California, even at a run-down motel, and in its plain bathroom, faced with the slaughter of Marion Crane (Janet Leigh), he did it daintily, fastidiously. He boasted piously that, in that shower scene in *Psycho*, you never saw a knife entering flesh. It was just that you thought you had seen it. And so, in an English way, the genteel and the gross stayed hand in glove.

The English have always had it within their imaginative refinement to do murders as cold-blooded, vicious, and mean-spirited as any in the world. It's not just Colonel Mustard in the conservatory with a candlestick. Shakespeare has that fearsome scene when assassins fall upon Lady Macduff and her child; he also laid down an interpretation for history in the killing of the princes in the Tower—a story that gave license to Laurence Olivier, Kevin Spacey, and many other actors in making Richard III a high-class pantomime villain. In Dickens, there are terrible murders, like Bill Sikes bludgeoning Nancy in *Oliver Twist*. This is the culture that produced *Dr. Jekyll and Mr. Hyde* (1886), Jack the Ripper (1888), and those oppressive paintings by Walter Sickert of the Camden Town murders (1908), in which the dark shape of a brutish man looms over a pale prostitute sprawled on a shabby bed in some wretched room. This is the breeding ground for such real monsters as Reginald Christie, the Moors murderers, Peter Sutcliffe, and Dr. Harold Shipman. That doctor had at least 250 victims in the late twentieth century, most of them his own patients. There was a TV movie, *Harold Shipman: Doctor Death* (2002), where James Bolam played Shipman. More than seven million people watched it. 7.3.

It's not safe in Britain.

On the other hand, many well-behaved readers and viewers have found comfort in a nice English murder. Take the career of Dame Agatha Christie (1890–1976), a well-born English woman of irreproachable reputation who became the best-selling mystery writer in the world. She wrote sixty-six novels, most of which start with murder, sometimes gruesome, but tactfully rendered and seen from a distance so that delicate readers need not be afraid or sickened. Agatha seldom entered into the minds or action of her murderers; instead she gloried in eccentric, talkative detectives like Hercule Poirot and Miss Marple. They made the calm of reading a consolation in times of turmoil. People on fire-watch in the Blitz read Agatha Christie in the glow of war. Some of those ladylike readers might be trapped in unkind domestic situations of their own, so they did embroidery or stamp collecting and read dainty tales of murder as a diversion.

Fearful souls are fond of good thrillers. The proposal that murders can be "solved" is very conservative. Miss Christie did not tolerate doubt. Yet the police will tell you that many of these whodunits remain open (we still don't agree who killed the Black Dahlia in 1947 in Los Angeles). Even then it is one thing to identify a killer and something far more searching to understand why the killings occurred. So why did Nicole Simpson die in Los Angeles in 1994? To take things a step further: why does that city sometimes erase beautiful lost women? Is that a cultural overflow from the movies made there?

Two billion Agatha Christie books have been purchased, in translations into more than a hundred languages. A play she wrote, *The Mousetrap*, opened at the Ambassadors Theatre in London in 1952—and it is still playing (like Elizabeth II). There is no getting away from the stereotype of an elderly English lady, in a durable tweed suit, going into a bookshop and asking for a gentle murder story. Those ladies and their bookshops are harder to find these days. But the franchise goes on and on. Late in 2017, the erstwhile radical actor-director Kenneth Branagh delivered an unbelievably bad film of *Murder on the Orient Express* (far worse than the Sidney Lumet original from 1974) in which he was himself fleetingly visible behind a hedge of mustache as

Hercule Poirot. This film was not laughed off the screen; it earned $350 million; *Death on the Nile* was announced as a follow-up for 2020.

If only to wave the honorable flag of bad taste, I wonder whether John Reginald Christie, a notable London murderer in the postwar era, and the killer of at least eight people, was not inspired or provoked by having the same name as the past-mistress of that mystery genre. Reg Christie was vile: he strangled timid souls and buried their corpses in and around his home in Notting Hill, in the walls and in the yard. His story was told in the movie *10 Rillington Place*, in which Richard Attenborough was a very creepy Christie. Reg was hanged in 1953, but the public still shudders with delight over his sordid story. In 2016, Tim Roth repeated the role for BBC television.

Alfred Hitchcock never filmed Agatha Christie material; I suspect he felt himself tougher in his attitudes, more rigorous in his treatment of killing, more grown-up, as well as a man of a distinctly lower class than Christie's. But Alfred and Agatha were contemporaries in the cultivated dread of being killed, and they are names that most of us would place under the rubric of "entertaining murders." Hitch never quite lost an Englishness that Miss Christie took for granted as something a lady could not get rid of.

Alfred was born in unfashionable Leytonstone to the east of London in 1899, the son of a greengrocer. The family lived in a flat above the shop. They were never poor, but they went into London to earn a better living. Agatha was the daughter of Frederick Miller, an American stockbroker, who had moved to England. She was born in Torquay in Devon, a seaside resort for affluent people, and she grew up there in a fine villa, in comfort and happiness—that was her own estimate. Alfred was not unhappy, but he was never as sure of himself. He was a lonely boy, a devout Catholic, famously afraid of getting into trouble. In the time of the Great War, he was classified C3, which meant he was fit only for sedentary work. He was overweight and unathletic. He could not think of himself as attractive, and he remembered having no friends. He grew up alone in the room of his own watchfulness.

What has this got to do with murder? Please consider: few are going to get into the wickedness of taking other lives without some humble dissatisfaction with their own existence. Tom Ripley prefers to be Dickie Greenleaf; Dr. Jekyll is tempted to become Mr. Hyde; and so many killers regard themselves as actors—the limelight can burn away guilt. Harry Lime is quite horrid, but he is known for his style, his wit, and Orson Welles's sly, self-adoring smile.

Hitch finished official schooling by the age of fifteen. But he did night classes, studying engineering, and that improved his talent for drawing plans, forms, and shapes in space. That is the core of his astonishing art: he was a confirmed planner, and he would become famous for movies haunted by suspenseful spaces derived from his meticulous storyboards. He liked things in order. The best biographies of the man suggest that he was a virgin when he met Alma Reville. They were both at work by then in the British film industry, and Alma was a little ahead of Alfred as a scriptwriter. They would marry and have a daughter, born in 1928. Alma became a vital aide and adviser to Alfred, deferring to him, and it is a question of critical interest as to how she accommodated his rapt gaze for pretty women and enchanting actresses. He adored Ingrid Bergman, and watching her (they made three films together). No evidence suggests that Alfred ever had sex with anyone but Alma. (Not in life, but that genre did not impress him as much as cinema.) If he had slept around, he might not have been the intense filmmaker. Had he been one of the lads, he might not have contemplated murder so much.

So Hitchcock began to make films in the silent era when visual design was more obviously important than it is now. He was drawn to "thrillers" or mystery films. He was a student of the films Fritz Lang was making in Germany—he copied shots and situations from *Dr. Mabuse the Gambler* (1922). But Germany was set on its grim destiny while Hitch was operating in the cheery culture of Miss Christie's books: her first hit, *The Mysterious Affair at Styles* (the name of a rich country house), had been published in 1920. Her offstage violence was not just in response to censorship, but part of a general sensibility in those English days that violence should not be a pressing or central reality. Keep it eccentric and nearly playful. So killings were done discreetly, quickly, and politely—to be offensive or forcefully real could endanger the loyalty of the audience and its wish to keep such urges repressed. There was a pathology in that secrecy, and

Hitchcock struggled with it all his life. Sometimes such smothered conflict can make a person murderous.

So there are murders in early Hitchcock. *The Lodger* (1927) is about a killer in the tradition of Jack the Ripper. *Blackmail*, his first sound picture, turns on a threatened woman stabbing a would-be rapist: its detail is clear, though the sound stress on the word "Knife!" is more striking. There was even a film called *Murder!* (1930), which Alma Reville scripted. A vein of cold misanthropy was emerging: it's there in Peter Lorre's assassin in *The Man Who Knew Too Much* (1934). But Hitch could be a tease. He had a coup in *The 39 Steps* (from the John Buchan novel) in which there is a swift knife-in-the-back murder, which is less memorable than the passage where Robert Donat and Madeleine Carroll are on the run, handcuffed together, so that when she removes her stockings his hands have to go along with hers. Hitch was as sexually alert as a killer waiting for a chance. (He invented that woman character and the handcuffing—Buchan never thought of her.) His biggest hit, *The Lady Vanishes* (1938), full of sinister humor, might have been written by Christie.

There is one startling murder in English Hitchcock, like a beast getting free. *Sabotage* (1936) is based on Joseph Conrad's novel *The Secret Agent*. Oscar Homolka plays a London cinema owner, Karl Verloc, who is also a bomb-making anarchist, with Sylvia Sidney as his wife. Her young brother—a child, Stevie— lives with them, and Verloc sends the boy to deliver a package (secretly a bomb timed to go off). But the boy is delayed; the bomb explodes and he is killed. Mrs. Verloc realizes this and there follows an intense domestic scene where in loathing of her husband she picks up a kitchen knife and . . .

The scene is a montage of fragments, faces, and the knife—Sylvia Sidney hated the many isolated close-ups that she felt kept her from acting. But when edited, the situation was so complex and compelling. Does Verloc will his own death? Does his wife murder him? We are left in uncertainty and in admiration for a scene that lets us identify with both characters. Hitch's movies are always obsessed with cinema, but his motifs are sex and murder (and their marriage).

The remarkable thing in *Sabotage* is that the rapid editing does not eliminate a contemplative air—the participants are thinking about murder and death in voluntary and involuntary action. The thought of murder is as pregnant as the knife. For Hitchcock had an intuition about murder as a taboo longing, and he stayed English because he honored the struggle between smothered desire and the melodramatic fury of enactment. That is a definition of cinema itself.

The Hitchcock family moved to America in 1939 to make *Rebecca*, a story not just overshadowed by but haunted by the death of the title character, which was really a suicide. But the film hinges on the way her husband, Maxim (Laurence Olivier), might have killed Rebecca, because he hated her so much. That silent mantra we repeat to ourselves—"I could kill you"—is often lurking in Hitchcock. But for years his preoccupation with murder held back from showing it.

Then, in *Shadow of a Doubt* (1943), Joseph Cotten plays a serial killer who longs to be good old Uncle Charlie for his dull, bourgeois family in Santa Rosa, California (which seems a cozy and English place). He has done horrific things (near New York), but we do not see them, and we understand why his Californian niece, another Charlie (Teresa Wright), feels close to him. The uncle is so much more alert than humdrum Santa Rosa, where her father and his friend mull over reported murders like armchair connoisseurs. But when she begins to uncover the uncle's secret, he thinks to kill her in self-protection. Charlie kills Charlie? Murder as suicide? The film is a masterpiece without one shown murder. But its death wish lets us feel why these two characters have the same name.

It was as if the fearful, respectable Alfred was edging his way closer to ugly acts. *Rope* (1948) is sometimes hailed as a step forward, but I think it is no such thing. It is derived from Patrick Hamilton's play, which in turn owed a lot to the Leopold and Loeb case. In 1924, those outstanding students at the University of Chicago had carried out a murder as an intellectual exercise. That is a promising direction to pursue, but it undercuts Hitch's stifled passion—that of intuiting that law-abiding people can want someone dead. In *Rope* the young men have no drive beyond a vague homosexual alliance. And so the film is a moribund stage play, shot in bewildering ten-minute takes. The exercise is reduced to technical fuss.

Strangers on a Train is so aware of motivation and duplicity it masks implausibility. Guy does want his wife disposed of, so maybe his weakness lets Bruno do the deed. Complicity is a deep topic, and it fits with the way movies can act out our guilty longings. Patricia Highsmith was so much more knowing about psychology than Agatha Christie, and she had iron in her soul.

By the 1950s Hitchcock's shy murderous instinct was emerging, and it was allied to his looking at women with a desire that might lead to attack. *Dial M for Murder* has a silly convoluted plot, but it blooms in its imagery of Grace Kelly under threat. Her husband, Tony (Ray Milland), has hired a stranger to murder Margot (he needs her money, but he wants revenge—for she has had an affair). She answers the phone late one evening, in her nightdress—it is her husband calling from his alibi club dinner—and as she takes the call the assassin comes out of the dark to throttle her with a stocking. It is a frightening scene in which her hand reaches out and finds a pair of scissors to stick in her murderer's back. Hitchcock loved knives—it's not easy to think of a film where he employs a gun. The blade is more cinematic and more intimate.

Rear Window (1954) involves a murder done with household knives, but we never see it. Instead, across the way in a Greenwich Village courtyard, Jeff and Lisa (James Stewart and Kelly) pick up on the circumstantial signs of a middle-aged man killing his nagging wife in an ugly marriage. *Rear Window* plays out against a survey of marital relations that is funny yet jaundiced, even if the Jimmy and Grace characters will end up together. But Lisa is nearly murdered in pursuit of the truth—and Jeff has let it happen and Hitch is thrilled by her peril.

It would have been Grace in *Vertigo* (1958), but Hitchcock had let her meet a prince in Monaco during the making of *To Catch a Thief*. So Kim Novak had the part in *Vertigo*'s story of two murders, though one we never see and the other can be read as an unfortunate accident on the spur of a far-fetched moment. But within the psychological turmoil of *Vertigo* there is a riddle about the mixed feelings a director can have for an actress—he loves her yet he's going to kill her.

Suppose the shy or repressed genius was inching towards a kind of confession. Grant that the climate of censorship was beginning to break down so that vivid violence was emerging from the shell of constraint. *Psycho* was coming. And that is a film, fifty-nine years old as I write, yet so well known there's no need to recount its story. So let me describe it in a way more suited to what was a strange and disconcerting ritual in 1960. It was less a story than an enactment, or an experiment in furtive desire.

In a cheap hotel room in Phoenix, Arizona, not in that state's traditional sunshine, but in harsh black and white, we find a couple who have had a lunchtime fuck. Fucking in 1960 was not what it is now; it was coming out of its closet. He, Sam Loomis (John Gavin), is twenty-nine; he is divorced and paying alimony; and he has a hardware store in northern California, in an invented town called Fairvale. She, Marion Crane (Janet Leigh), is thirty-three; she has not been married; and she is secretary to a real estate agent in Phoenix.

They are in love; they want to be together—so they say. There is no law impeding that. Their sexual act has occurred before the film begins at 2:43 in the Friday afternoon; it seems to have been adequate, if constrained, and it did not end in sleep. Later in the film Sam drafts a letter to her saying, why not get married? "So what if we're poor and cramped and miserable, at least we'd be happy!" There must be hardware stores in Phoenix, or openings for secretaries in Fairvale. He owes alimony still for a few years (he says), but are moviegoers seeing lunchtime passion expected to believe in that caution? Or is there some unseen obstacle, some fear of marriage, some reticence over going all that way? People in movies, for decades, had gone on wild sprees of escape and liberty. This weird hesitation helps define *Psycho* as Hitchcock's first resolutely American film, filled with social anxiety about being free. Voyeurs are prisoners in their privileged dark.

It is key to *Psycho* that Janet Leigh comes to us stretched out on the bed like a prize or a whore. It's as if the sex hasn't quite happened yet—she does not seem satisfied. If the scene were filmed today, Marion would probably be naked. But in 1960, Leigh was wearing a white slip and a white bra. That made her more desirable—and she was very attractive. Still, there was an inescapable implication that she went with the hotel room; that she never took off the bra or the slip; that they were part of her professionalism. The film didn't have the warmth to show that she was dreamy or in a rapture from the recent sex—it must have occurred between 2:00 and 2:43. She isn't even untidy. Her hair has not been messed. She's sexuality being filmed and as candid as 1960 could be—but that amounts to a confession over movies and 1960, and a hint that Hitch's sensuality was raging but frigid.

The film moves on. Marion goes back to her office (her co-worker there is played by the Hitchcocks' daughter, Patricia, as a shallow gossip). The Friday afternoon involves a cash transaction in the office. An older man in a cowboy hat whose eyes explore Marion lecherously is buying a property for $40,000 in cash. Marion's nervous boss wants her to deposit the money in the bank immediately. So she gets off early.

She goes back to where she lives and changes her clothes. Is that necessary, or is it that Hitch wants to see it? She puts on a black bra now—and we can see it, though it's not clear what we are doing there. That may sound a foolish remark about a movie, but why is the scene being shown to us? Answer that question and you have a certain moral stance, because, just as we see Marion in her underwear again, a touch more seductive in black, we realize that she is thinking of stealing the money. There is a lengthy silent sequence where we share in this stealth. We know she's being foolish, but we want her to do it. And her undress is like mood music or assistance. Her transgression is a sexual act.

There is then an extended passage, stretching over more than twenty-four hours, in which Marion drives north to Fairvale. She sleeps in her parked car one night and the voices of people in her head torment her with the realization that stealing $40,000 was madness. Albeit a madness lived out in practical, paranoid control. It starts to rain; day turns to night. Head on in the camera's remorseless scrutiny, with a back projection of distance unwinding behind her, Marion stops at a motel. She has been grilled on this journey by the movie process and by our watching. She is a bad girl, but so vulnerable; she is sitting there alone, like us, locked in unknown rapport.

It's still Janet Leigh, lovely and wholesome, and seemingly full of common sense, no matter how foolish she has been. And filling out that underwear. We sympathize with her, we do. But we want her (this does suppose the film had been made for men—is it against women in the sweet guise of adoring them?).

You know what follows. You don't have to be advised that it was the most devastating murder scene in American film. Nor is it less than horrific still. I saw the first public screening in London in a nearly deserted Plaza cinema and I was begging the frenzy to stop. So it was a great relief when Norman Bates (Anthony Perkins) came into the fevered motel cabin, felt the horror, and began to clean up, to restore calm. But it was also true that on the brink of the shower Marion had taken off all her clothes. We did not see her exactly naked, not even in the shower, but there was a feeling of release. And then the knife came in.

The shower slaughter was compulsive; it was an eruption of desire. But it was fanatically controlled and organized. I said that Hitch was a planner, and this minute of screen time had taken five days to shoot—not just the sequence of so many brief shots, but the assembling of a complex sound track, all the way from shots of Marion as a madonna in the fall of water to that necrophiliac view of her sprawled out of the shower, a still life with one open eye. It was a revolution in which the contemplation of raw horror had become a masterwork. Decency was slipping away with the blood and the shower water.

Hitchcock had been afraid of *Psycho* in a businesslike way. His home studio, Paramount, thought it would prove disgusting, the opposite of entertaining, so the project was moved over to Universal. Then it was set up on a low budget—that explained the black and white—using a crew that Hitchcock had waiting from his television show. Paramount's fear was not fulfilled. The movie was the greatest success Hitch would ever have: it cost $800,000 and took in $50 million in a first swallow. The picture outraged some people, but it became world famous, and was seized upon by those who had reckoned for years that Hitch was a genius instead of just an entertainer. Moreover, the outrage in *Psycho* encouraged others. It indicated where cinema was going, and should be going—away from censorship, and into an erotic and violent candor allegedly suitable for grown-up people. Few films have had more influence on other filmmakers, or so promised an onset of horror as a significant genre. You can argue that these things would have happened anyway, but that cheats the dangerous originality of *Psycho*.

Alfred Hitchcock had done well for two decades in America. As well as the films mentioned so far, he had made *Foreign Correspondent, Suspicion, Notorious, The Wrong Man,* and *North by Northwest*. He was famous enough by 1960 to be the promotional tool for *Psycho*, a presence in the trailer—fat, lugubrious, poker-faced, clerical but sinister—that imitated his appearances on his TV show. He was rich now, and supreme in his way. Yet he had never won an Oscar for directing, or had a grand affair with one of his actresses. This was in a profession where some directors had done both. So English Alfred, the lower-class boy, felt overlooked. And truly, his lack of an Oscar was ridiculous (he and Janet Leigh were nominated for *Psycho*, but not Anthony Perkins!). It was enough to suggest that he was disdained or to make him feel closer to Norman, that archetypal kid alone in his room.

This is supposition, but suppose he was aggrieved and hurt—a stiff upper lip is a kind of hard-on. In the course of his next films, *The Birds* and *Marnie*, Hitchcock urged himself upon his new actress, Tippi Hedren. She was thirty-two, he was sixty-three. He was obese and he was aging, and it's possible that he felt he was closer to power than he had ever come before. As Hedren reported it, their private scenes were ugly and embarrassing. She rejected his advances and that must have devastated Hitchcock's love of secrecy.

He was not the same again as a director, no matter that tributes like François Truffaut's book-length interview placed him as the essential film director. Moreover, the onset of nakedness and blood in movies from the late sixties on—the industrialization of murder to a point of pornography—often hailed him as a godfather figure, even if Hitch himself was shocked by the changes.

Some directors who had survived censorship and flourished under its silly rules (like Howard Hawks and Billy Wilder) were taken aback to realize how much could be put on the new screen.

Hitch was more conservative than they were, still naturally secretive and English—in *The Birds*, for instance, amid the mayhem of a bird attack at Bodega Bay there appears an old lady ornithologist, wearing tweeds and speaking in sentences, who could be an Agatha Christie detective. Hitch always liked to dine and wine in the style of an English country gentleman.

Then he sought to sum it all up. He was seventy-two when he went back to London to make *Frenzy* (1972), an unholy conflict of forces. Its killer works in the greengrocery trade. But its murder is hideously ill-judged: it has a rape and a strangling in which the cruelty feels out of control. It's the work of an Englishman who does not realize how hard it is to regain the decorum and the wit of his 1930s thrillers. As if challenged by the cinematic liberties of *The Godfather* or *Last Tango in Paris*, his voyeurism is a cold stare. *Frenzy* is a bad movie and an uncomfortable experience, but it concludes Hitchcock's arc and underlines the perils in his obsession with murder.

He struggled with his cruel instincts for years. That suppressed torment is a plea in his work. But *Psycho*'s dynamic swayed many younger directors, some of whom were more complacent about cruelty. Brian De Palma's *Dressed to Kill* (1980) likes to see itself as a sardonic exercise. A well-groomed woman of a certain age, Kate (Angie Dickinson), is presented as an emblem of unfulfilled desire. She tries to seduce her shrink (Michael Caine). When he refuses her, she picks up a stranger in the Metropolitan Museum of Art and lets him take her home to bed.

The stalking in the Met, the urbane Upper East Side sex, and her discovery that this man has a sexually transmittable disease are done with gloating precision. The erotic suspense is shaded by a superior, if not supercilious, amusement. But then as Kate leaves her uneasy tryst, she steps into an elevator and is fatally razor-slashed by a mysterious female figure.

The filming is meticulous and poised—it was treated with critical reverence. But few seemed to notice the human indifference: the killer was so far from Norman Bates, and the bourgeois Kate lacked the fraught warmth of Janet Leigh's Marion. It was as if murder had come to resemble engineering: if it worked smoothly the personal consequences could be set aside.

It's clearer now that De Palma was an accomplished engineer, while Hitchcock was as tortured a creative force as Van Gogh. Handling murder really is a severe test of one's feeling for life.

Which guides us to warfare, sometimes hailed as explosions of political desire, but equally susceptible to the vagary of a season. Like shooting grouse from August 12 onwards (until December 12). It was at that season in 1914 that the various parties picked sides and agreed to have a war.

THE GOOD SOLDIER

War is a very bad thing—we say that every time it happens. But it does seem to be a social habit, so perhaps we should consider how far we enjoy it and set it up. Most wars become "official"; they are "declared"; and then some common codes of decency are suspended. Men realize they are freer to behave badly, and there have been wars in which the hallowed Geneva conventions have been forgotten. Murder can run riot over talk of strategy or "decisiveness." Bravery itself falters ideologically in the face of ordinary cowardice and compromise.

In the television documentary *The Vietnam War*, by Ken Burns and Lynn Novick, it is steadily conceded that official, "permitted" combat killing was one thing, and the casual offing of civilians, or "the wrong gooks," was another, not to be confused with GIs sometimes disposing of zealous officers who insisted on one damn attack after another. Still, there will always be a conservative interpretation of military killing that regards it as men's work, a duty that will let guys be all that they can be.

Is war where men are tested? Or is it just a field of endeavor where murder is permitted, taught, and honed to an expensive art? The era of the Great War was tormented with earnest explanations of why and how that war had to be fought. But in the exhausted aftermath it was hard to count the uncontrolled and inadequately clerked slaughter of four years in which armies and nations had been sleepwalking in the dream of killing and being killed.

What is the freedom being fought for when doomed men are so ready to go under orders? Is freedom itself being murdered? There is a large painting by John Singer Sargent, *Gassed* (1919), 90 inches by 240, that shows a single file of soldiers, hands on shoulders, shuffling towards a dressing station on the western front. But these men hold on to one another because they are blind from mustard gas; they cannot see where they are going, or the spectacle they make. The painting has become a model of that war, and a rueful commentary on maintaining a disciplined military line. The picture came from Sargent's visit to the front lines in the summer of 1918, and it is housed in London's Imperial War Museum where boys still go to imagine soldiering.

Another line of uniformed men is walking across sunlit fields. They are not blind; they still have unit structure; they have to believe they are advancing, as in getting on and knowing where they are—but the lucid vision of this film understands that walking may be self-sufficient. The actual fields we see were in Malibu Canyon, Thousand Oaks Ranch, and Bronson Canyon, but the movie says we are somewhere in Korea. The entire film is in the open air and it feels like a fine place for a walk.

This movie appeared in 1957, and it is called *Men in War*, written by Philip Yordan and directed by Anthony Mann. To this day, Mann has had no equal as a filmmaker in love with open country, its articulate spaces, and the variety of trees, grasses, and earth that exist there. For the most part he is famous for Westerns in which his preoccupation with land and distance is dressed up in the prim moral codes of the Western genre—the stuff about honor, duty, courage, and making America a better place. But Mann was a poet who knew landscape was a wonder that had no faith in improvement or justification. *Men in War* is his great film because the land is its basis, and if you haven't heard of the film, that is proof that a wonder can exist in cinema history that is no more remarked on than the splendor of that tree over there, that oak.

Estimates place 7.3 billion trees in California alone, give or take 100 million.

This is an American patrol walking in Korea, an infantry platoon with instructions to take a numbered hill. It is led by a Lieutenant Benson (played by Robert Ryan), humane and conscientious but unsure of his role—he is a forerunner of Tom Hanks's Captain Miller in *Saving Private Ryan* (1998), someone doing his best while unconvinced that any scheme of best or not best really exists. The 1957 film rarely sees the enemy, but North Koreans are there—they order down artillery bombardments, they have planted land mines, and they can be the silent outlier who snakes through the grass and knifes one soldier, Killian (James Edwards), who seeks the relief of sitting down to take off his boots for a moment and puts wild flowers on his helmet. We see his bare foot stiffen and then the grass shiver as his killer gets away. It's a death, a loss, but it's a knockout scene.

The unit is losing its members by attrition. But then it encounters a shell-shocked colonel and a sergeant who cares for his helpless leader. The sergeant, "Montana," is played by Aldo Ray—as an antithesis to Ryan, he is an aggressive warrior, on the edge of being brutal and ruthless. Benson is weaker or more compromised; he is a decent man who wants the war over. For Montana, combat is his element, the thing he has been waiting for.

Montana's attitude threatens Benson's command. After Killian's death, Montana sits down on a trail and pretends to sleep. When that lures a Korean assassin, he savagely bayonets the enemy. Later, it is Montana who resorts to a kind of secret or extra weapon, a flamethrower, that achieves victory in the film's small local conflict. Crude flamethrowers had been used as early as the Great War, and they were common in the Second, but in 1957 they were a novelty in film, and Anthony Mann seemed awed by the blooms of fire that leaped across the land and the screen. They were drastic and beautiful as only black-and-white could manage. In color, flame would have been less austere or exemplary. Color may have been depleting for murder. Red blood can seem more real, but often its hues remind us of the fakery involved. Black blood can be so much more poetic.

At the end of *Men in War,* Benson and Montana toss medals down a burned hillside and recite the names of the dead. But the sergeant has surpassed the lieutenant, and the film concedes that we are going to have to destroy anybody in our way—they might be soldiers, they might be peasant bystanders. As we know from later Asian wars, there was not always time to distinguish one from the other. Didn't they all look alike? Didn't a flamethrower or napalm need to take them all out, as well as every tree? If you doubt the screen power of a flamethrower, see what Tarantino did with an antique wand of incineration in *Once Upon a Time . . . in Hollywood.*

Aged sixteen, I was thrilled by *Men in War,* and I have admired it ever since. But as I write this book, as I see myself or any watcher sitting there alone, there is more to say. Some soldiers die in the film, but tastefully. There is nothing like the shattered bodies in *Saving Private Ryan.* Nineteen fifty-seven was so much more genteel, and so unaware that movie audiences would soon feast on slaughter. That seems sheltered now. But it only points at the weird security of the spectator.

Anthony Mann was thirty-five when the war broke out for America, and he did not serve. That is not a challenge to his reputation, but it is a way of saying that the best combat films tend to be made by noncombatants. Fixing up a battle scene, with makeup, stage blood, props, controlled explosions, and corpses, can seem in poor taste if you've been there and remember what an unholy mess battle was. And then the lies.

It was not tidy, let alone elegant, and it is both the quality and a limitation of *Men in War* that it is so beautiful. My teenage pleasure was that of an armchair soldier who was praying that he could avoid national service. There is a troubling dynamic between the screen's frenzy and our sitting there all alone. How else could cinema work? you ask. What else is reading but the adjacency of our intense privacy and, say, the battle of Borodino in *War and Peace,* or Lo and Hum at the Enchanted Hunters motel in *Lolita?* It has to be, but that is no reason to ignore how far the experiences of film and reading do cultivate selfhood, separation, and selfishness. We like to think we are "involved" and in sympathy with what we see. But we are safe, reflective, and rather cold. It would be so different if the men on screen stepped forward, their flamethrowers scathing our eyes.

I am using war as a pretext here. My purpose is to have you ask how you watch so many murders with the distance of a connoisseur or a general on a hilltop far away.

Murder is a crime, a sin, it is ugly, and it's a practice you warn your children about and hope to be protected against. But killing can be something else. It is what you will do to protect yourself, your family, and even innocent parties against what may be improper attack. It is what policemen may be pushed to in a crisis—or in what they judge to be a crisis. Killing can be self-defense, so maybe if you're worried you could think of striking first? Self-protection becomes politics.

Military personnel are trained and equipped, and sent out to operate under the rubric of duty or orders. There is a mission: that hill, that village, that possible area of uncertainty, needs to be "taken" or cleared. Its uncertainty has to be ended. The military members are directed by officers, and killing comes more comfortably when responsibility and choice are erased. The pressure of combat should be unambiguous. And so some fighting men and women may have killed large numbers of the enemy, along with some innocent bystanders. That bargain has to be made, and it tends to eliminate the concept of "innocent" as superfluous or sentimental; "unlucky" may be a better word.

It's natural to think that war films, or combat stories, are about the people involved in the crises. But if you step back a moment, and just consider the titles, it's easier to wonder whether they are not songs about the weapons, or the dehumanized atmosphere of warfare, and warnings about what to expect. There is another Anthony Mann film—*Winchester 73* (1950)—and you can say it's about Jimmy Stewart being a good guy. But could it also be the story of a weapon circling through the 1870s in the West? The list of such titles is longer than I have time for: *Colt .45* (1950); *Springfield Rifle* (1952); *Gun Crazy* (1950); *Gunfight at the O.K. Corral* (1957) . . . so many of these films seem like boyish adventures, but then the zone becomes more intense or less interested in people, as if it understood the ethos of weaponry in America:

In the Line of Fire (1993); *The Hurt Locker* (2008); *Point Blank* (1967). I love that last film, by John Boorman, with Lee Marvin as an outlaw trying to get the $93,000 he is owed. But its title has no obvious link to his character or the story. It's the sort of title that the industry thought fit and commanding, as if to say some deadly force was at hand, some killing machine. What does *Kiss Me Deadly* (1955) mean? Or *American Sniper* (2014)—it's hard to imagine a picture called *British Sniper*—not that there aren't such trained fellows waiting at a thousand yards in the queen's name.

The armory is as steadily promoted as in advertisements for the National Rifle Association. It's as if the gun had a life of its own, or an authority and a drama that eclipsed the person holding it. This happens in the pursuit of a necessary mission, to protect . . . you know the rest. You've heard it in so many war movies or in commercials for the Marines or the Army—and you would hardly know the rules of war but for movies. Without cinema you might decide that war was chaos, appalling wounds, devastating betrayals of decency and honor, and results that mock all the set purposes spelled out in grand speeches about war aims. German soldiers after 1945 said they had been obeying orders, so then we asked that soldiery be capable of cross-examining orders.

Soldiers may resent that much philosophy. Sooner or later, a line of men must cross a dangerous field. Look at *1917*.

A military life—its scheme—can override so much uneasiness. In all the purposes of war don't underestimate its offer to assuage the ordinary terror of young men. Never mind death, they have so much to fear in the way of living. They are alarmed at the prospect of being without parental care or presence; they dread the thought of not having that embrace and its guidance. They suspect they know too little; they have not been educated to think for themselves; and so that selfhood feels out of reach. They do not know what to "do in life," or how to get ahead and make a living. They wonder whether they will become derelicts or outlaws—or miserable successes. They do not know how to reconcile their sexual urges—that helpless manufacturing of desire—with the test of talking to women, of being with them in dispute or conversation over what manliness should mean (or how foolish it may be).

And in that turmoil they long for certainty and a system in which men are obeyed—even young, ill-educated men who know too little and who are terrified by their ignorance. They are haunted by all those fears, and they would like to kill them, as in remove them, put them out of mind so they might awake—in the darkness before dawn—and feel secure. Killing is not only an act of extreme prejudice aimed against other men, it is a denial of too much difficulty or doubt in oneself. More or less, young men join a military life because doubt is taken away by a uniform, a corps of men in which individuality is smoothed out, and intimidated personality is subsumed in the unifying ontology of a corpus as well as a corpse, in which murder is permitted and encouraged.

Look at a film about a group of young men—a gang—trained and sent thousands of miles to murder a young woman. You can complain that that is no adequate way to describe *Full Metal Jacket*—a film about a bullet. But my caption is instructive; it reaches the poetry of the film, its secret sense about irrational male groupings.

Made in 1987, *Full Metal Jacket* was scripted by Michael Herr and Gustav Hasford and taken from Hasford's novel *The Short-Timers*, but it is a Stanley Kubrick film. Kubrick never did military service: he was unfit in the way smart young men—geniuses included—have managed to be spared. Don't they have a duty to stay alive in their room? Yet he was obsessed with male groupings and their struggles with fear and disorder: *Fear and Desire* was about a military patrol; *Paths of Glory* depicts a prison system called an army; *Spartacus* longs for an army of freed slaves; *Dr. Strangelove* is a satire on duty; *2001* is soldiers in space, who surrender character to their technology; and then there is *Full Metal Jacket*.

Born in 1928, Stanley was an impressionable teenager horny over photos in the age of the great just conflict—the Second World War—when the "free world" and brave young men came together in a test that had to be fought, and which was inherently justified. We still tell that story. Without it, the malign force of Adolf Hitler and authoritarianism, with its allies in Japan and Italy, could have destroyed humanity. So be it. That war was fought and it's easier to live with this weary answer: let's say "we" won it. But was humanity saved? Or were its prospects reduced? It was part of that interpretation of living history and its litany of death that we grew up on valiant team films like *The Story of*

G.I. Joe, A Walk in the Sun, Battleground, Sands of Iwo Jima, Men in War, and so on. This is a line that could include *From Here to Eternity,* and even *Saving Private Ryan,* often considered one of the best films about the chaos and the technological reality of that just war, and of the legend that individuals were required to honor the justice, and the sacrifice of it all, as a way of deserving life.

Full Metal Jacket is as remorseless and as cold as the proof of a theorem. It takes a group of raw recruits and sees them being shaped as a unit. Kubrick does not bother much with accuracy. Blithely, he found his Vietnam locations in Britain. With the same indifference, he overlooked the reality of American military service in Vietnam being the realm of kids, no more than twenty-two, with a preponderance of black men. In the cast for *Full Metal Jacket,* Matthew Modine was twenty-eight, Arliss Howard was thirty-three, Adam Baldwin was twenty-five, Vincent d'Onofrio was twenty-eight, and Dorian Harewood (the notable black actor in the group) was thirty-seven.

This casting brought recognizable acting personality to a challenging commercial project. It also infused the group with more critical eloquence than we'd find in uneducated kids from the rural hinterland or the deprived suburbs of America's distracted and sometimes ruined cities—the real base for the 58,000 who were killed in our cause in Vietnam. I don't complain at that: the choice highlights Kubrick's plan to confound young intelligence or optimism.

Full Metal Jacket comes in two tidy parts: in the first, a group of novices are made into a fighting unit. This is basic training, the military fundamentals, and a way of conforming the men as base humanity. They are drilled, humbled, made uniform as human individuality turns into the hard steel required of war. Their inept and flawed bodies are dressed in a full metal jacket called code; they become bullets.

This is accomplished, but there is a sacrificial victim, a hopeless case. His name is Leonard Lawrence but he is nicknamed Gomer Pyle (as played by Vincent D'Onofrio). It was during the bitter years of the Vietnam War that a character named Gomer Pyle (played by Jim Nabors) was presented as a comic figure, a doofus drafted into service, in the television series *Gomer Pyle USMC* (1964–69). He had been introduced first as a garage mechanic on *The Andy Griffith Show* (1962–64), and he was enjoyed as a dope, a man yet unmanly, a beloved figure of fun, enough to make Nabors a recognizable fellow in the panorama of provincial America.

The name Pyle also referred us back to Ernie Pyle (1900–1945), a newspaper writer who had reported on the experience of common soldiers in war. He lived in the front lines, and he was killed by machine-gun fire on a small island off Okinawa in April 1945. He was the basis for the film *The Story of G.I. Joe* (released in July 1945), in which Burgess Meredith plays Pyle as a tough but warm journalist admired by the grunts he described well enough to win a Pulitzer Prize. That film was intent on presenting the "reality" of war and it is still worth seeing, though it has a brave, limited view of war and service that won the approval of the military and did nothing to distract kids in the audience from signing up.

The Pyle in *Full Metal Jacket* is regarded without sentimentality. He is overweight, close to stupid, and a constant defaulter in the group. Some other recruits try to help him, but he is fiercely abused by the drill sergeant who runs the recruits (Lee Ermey) and who is a model fascistic leader set on eradicating human idiosyncrasy. This sergeant would like Pyle out of the group because he is an offense and an impossibility. In fact, Pyle does graduate, and he has learned more than enough to qualify. He takes his rifle and its bullets. He shoots and kills his sergeant and then he puts the gun to his own forehead and fires. Kubrick observes this without comment, but as if showing a logical consequence of basic training applied to a misfit. It is Pyle's duty to remove himself, and it is vengeance to take his hated sergeant with him. We loathe that sergeant, too, but we know that Pyle was beyond the conventional affection we felt for the wistful rebel of Montgomery Clift's Prewett in *From Here to Eternity*.

Without further ado, the film transports us and its unit to Vietnam, and to a very effective display of that war-torn country, even if it was arranged at the abandoned Beckton Gasworks in east London, with the tactful application of a few tattered palm trees and some Asian extras. Our men are there and they encounter the first females in the film: Vietnamese whores, fierce and without a sentimental touch (far blunter than the gracious Donna Reed in *From Here to Eternity*). They bargain with the G.I.s over the going rate for fuck and suck, and are alien, animalistic, and available. No whore wins or identifies the heart of a soldier.

As the group makes its aimless way forward, it encounters opposition from somewhere in the ruined urban horizon. At first the soldiers believe this is "the enemy," as in a full force of Vietcong. But it is just a single sniper in one of those buildings, a sharpshooter who can pick out one uniform or another and reduce it to a puff of red membrane and cries of agony—the trained bodies are so easily shattered, and we appreciate the accuracy of this process. It is in the nature of our safe place in the dark to identify with the mechanism that chooses a subject, fixes on it, and "gets it." This applies to any close-up as much as the act of shooting someone. If a character is under stress or delight, hit us with the close-up. A secret satisfaction says "Yes!" at the hit, no matter the loss and the pain. This works in twin directions. We want the G.I.s to get the sniper just as we want the sniper to get them. Film is a system that shoots—the double meaning in the word is inescapable.

The sniper is efficient, a natural, or a superior being in its overlook. Several of our guys are killed—the death of Cowboy (Arliss Howard) is especially shocking and credible, though there had been no effort to make us "like" his character in the way we become attached to Tom Hanks's captain and the other guys in *Saving Private Ryan.*

But this sniper turns out to be a young woman, unnamed in the film but played by Ngoc Le. The American soldiers hate her, of course. Eventually they do shoot her, and she lies on the broken ground, stricken, helpless, but feral still in her contempt for the G.I.s. Kubrick generally was at a loss with females in his films—I have noted how he disdains Wendy in *The Shining*. But the girl sniper is the most intense woman he ever filmed in that she simply resists male interpretation of what has happened. She hisses out her fury and her hatred until Joker puts a merciful bullet in her, not just saving her from distress or further suffering, but removing her in the approved dictum—that a soldier can kill anybody, and think that signifies victory. You have to be a chump to be a soldier. That's what the gun whispers to you.

We watch this from our solitude. We may get the "antiwar" message, but we cannot shrug off the glamour of detachment and enforcement. Being that alone is precious, but we should not forget how gently these storytelling media foster authoritarianism as well as authorship.

WE CAN KILL ANYBODY

There are official armies, and then there are all of us, the rest of us. We think of armies as being composed to protect us. But sometimes we may have to do that work ourselves, unofficially.

Jean-Pierre Melville's *L'Armée des Ombres* (1969) is a story of the French Resistance and its heroic members. One of the group, Mathilde (Simone Signoret), has crucial knowledge required by the Gestapo. But the Nazis know enough to threaten her daughter, and so the group recognizes that Mathilde needs to die to keep her knowledge quiet. But she is averse to suicide. So her companions in the Resistance decide to murder her. They wait for her in their car. As she walks the street, they drive by and execute her. That simple, bleak sequence, and Mathilde's fatalistic attitude, catch the vulnerability of Resistance and its gambling with life and death. By the end of the war everyone in this shadow group has been executed, tortured to death, or committed suicide.

"Resistance" is usually a fine word, but we should attend to history. It was resistance that made the American Revolution, and also prompted the struggle in Algeria, the development of Vietnamese independence, and the prolonged conflict in Ireland. There are resistance movements all over the world, some of which may be buried by tyranny, dread, and force of arms. Even in the USA now it is possible to foresee a new resistance and wonder whether it could be Resistance. Should the Germans have resisted after 1939, or 1943? Would you have done that?

L'Armée des Ombres was not well received in France when it opened, because the film admired the figure of De Gaulle and in 1969 that sentiment was not fashionable. So Melville's haunting film did not come to America for another twenty years. So many obstacles face resistance.

Was that what Winston Churchill foresaw in 1940 when he sketched out the future of an invaded Britain having to fight on the beaches, the landing grounds, the fields and the streets, and in the hills . . . you know this speech from so many films and Churchills. And the new prime minister was looking beyond official armies. He was proposing to enlist all of Britain in a resistance movement (as if collaboration was unthinkable). Resistance can be the true crisis of war, coming after formal defeat and occupation, when uniforms are no protection and the polite rules of warfare have been abandoned. That's when an individual will have to step forward, when the soldier feels the lonely spirit of inescapable politics.

One novelty of the second war was the prolonged experience

of occupation and the choice of collaborating or resisting. That ordeal did a lot to undermine French confidence. The famous victors in the war, Britain and America, never shared in that worst test. So the happy West has not cared to imagine the rigors of a world that has lost its order or authority. The state of resistance, and the need for lethal survivor skills, could haunt us yet in landscapes where disasters of weather and economic collapse become what we now call "postapocalyptic," like the condition in Cormac McCarthy's novel *The Road*. The most frightening thing about "the end of the world" can be that it is not quite curtains for everyone.

Movies are preparing us for the fierceness of a person left alone in chaos.

Consider a young man who had been a Marine in the Second World War—he fought in the Pacific and was awarded the Navy Cross—but he looks slight and modest and he loves his family. He has come home, with nowhere else to go. His father is a businessman—this is in the New York area just after the war—and in the way of big business he has rivals and enemies who make the father an offer he shouldn't refuse. But the dad is old-fashioned, and he declines. Not long after that, his enemies nearly kill him on the streets. So the father is wounded; then in hospital, under care and police guard. One evening, the Marine son goes to the hospital to see his father and he discovers the guards have disappeared. Some malign plot is building.

You know this story, don't you? Isn't it part of your culture now, like a fairy tale? Isn't it your Veldt?

So the son becomes a guard. He is unarmed—he is just a tender civilian—but he holds his coat in a way to suggest he has a gun. The police chief arrives at the hospital—is he visiting, too?—and he beats up the son when that kid challenges him for neglect. The kid's face swells from the beating; he cannot speak clearly. But he is becoming Michael Corleone, and that is a dreadful assignment.

There were disputes over who should play Michael in *The Godfather* (1972), just as arguments gathered over nearly every role in the film. It seems comic now to think about it, but there were so many options to play Vito Corleone—it could have been Laurence Olivier, Robert Mitchum, Frank Sinatra, George C. Scott—or even Orson Welles! This is like contemplating the collapse of a landmark building. As for Michael, many parties to the deal wanted a tall, handsome hero. They considered Warren Beatty, Robert Redford, Ryan O'Neal, and James Caan. But Francis Coppola, the screenwriter and the director, struggling to be in charge of the big venture, was determined to have Al Pacino.

Pacino was five-foot-seven, and he could seem shorter in person, for he was a little hunched. He had the face of a saint, not a conqueror, and all he had done so far was play lyrical outcasts. He did not seem to have the presence of a leader. But Coppola guessed that Pacino could become Michael Corleone and bring something resolute and implacable to that transition. A killer instinct. We too are shy at the movies, sitting in our dark, when we want to be grand, brave and triumphant. Michael is an austere model for that aspiration, and he becomes a refined master of murder. He pulls off so complete a trick it is absurd that Pacino never won an Oscar in the part.

The Corleone family is shattered by the attack on Vito. He will live, but in a weaker state. To rally themselves, the survivors think of revenge. There is a family gathering (for the men) with a swirl of talk and bravado gestures involving Sonny Corleone, Tom Hagen, the supreme adviser, Clemenza, Tessio, and even Fredo Corleone. But as this talk goes on, Coppola's camera settles on the battered Michael, sitting alone in an armchair, resting—a semi-invalid. But as if Michael feels that fateful camera movement as much as we do, he says he will carry out the vengeance. "I'll kill them both," he tells the family quietly. He will take out the corrupt police captain, McCluskey, and the family's leading enemy, Virgil Sollozzo. There is laughter and surprise at what the college boy is dreaming. But Michael is clear about it, and though he is small he is strong. He is irresistible.

It will be a test for a young knight. Michael will take a meeting with McCluskey and Sollozzo. There is no suggestion that the son is going there to negotiate a new compromise for the criminal empire in America. He is going to kill the enemy. Of course, he will be searched for weapons, frisked by experts. So the Corleones need to establish which restaurant is arranged for the meeting—and then it is up to the ingenious Clemenza to place a gun there. All Michael has to do is go to the bathroom at a certain moment and find the gun—a loaded gun—that has been secured above the cistern in the john.

The plan works beautifully, and we love the ritualistic fulfill-ment of plans in movies. (Suppose, for a moment, that the gun is in the wrong place—and Michael can't find it. He turns frantic and *The Godfather* risks becoming a Jerry Lewis picture.)

Michael Corleone is about to emerge as the central dark hero of modern cinema. "Modern" has a bitter taste in the mouth, I know: *The Godfather* was forty-eight years ago—go back forty-eight years from 1972 and we are at 1924, with *The Jazz Singer* yet to be heard. *The Godfather* has reason to be considered an antique, but if it feels fresh—and it is still watched in amazing numbers, by veterans and first-timers—then consider its con-fused attitude to murder.

Michael is searched by McCluskey himself in the limousine taking them to Louis's restaurant. But this has been anticipated and makes us hushed, remote accomplices to Michael, ready to hate the bullying confidence of McCluskey (Sterling Hayden) and the insidious treachery of Sollozzo (Al Lettieri). The scene has the ominous chords of Nino Rota's score, and it will have inventive layered sound effects from Walter Murch. The quiet restaurant in the Bronx—it has the best veal in town, Sollozzo promises—does have one curious handicap. A subway train runs nearby, it may go beneath the restaurant itself, and as tension mounts so Murch will bring that roar into the room. It's not exactly the atmosphere made men might seek at the end of the day. Never mind, this is a movie—that's why we're just watch-ing instead of crying out to McCluskey and Sollozzo, "Oh, guys, please take care!"

Are you kidding? you say. Well, no, I'm not. McCluskey and Sollozzo are "bad" men, no doubt, and they are being played with the best surface sweep of character actors who know they have fifteen minutes to register. But they could be human beings, too. They may have innocent family members who will be devastated by the loss. Are you touched yet? More than that, in 2019, I suspect most readers of this book are nearly as opposed to capital punishment as they are to murder. We do not believe in taking the law into our own hands and killing bad people on the streets—do we? Wouldn't it be better if these two targets were charged, tried, convicted, and sent to Sing Sing? Yet we are ready to have them killed—in the name of the family, but in our name, too. Why not—aren't we part of the pact? Doesn't the very title—*The Godfather*—promise a perverse religious care for us?

The three men at the table talk—the villains have no one else around. Michael goes to the bathroom, after he has been searched again. The gun is there, its handle wrapped in tape. He leaves the bathroom, comes back to the table ready to pop the two guys. We are talking about a moment of movie majesty, with the subway howling in our ears. Yet Michael considers his options in an uncanny mix of fear, eagerness, and absurdism. Is he really going to do this?

He has to. He can't let us down. He can't be like Herman Melville's Bartleby, preferring not to do it—or to do anything. So Michael takes the gun from his pocket and shoots the two men in their foreheads. They collapse, one in his food, the other thrust back in his chair. The table tips over. The music soars in triumph. And Michael hurries away, remembering to drop the gun as Clemenza told him. He has another date, not just a getaway, for he is going to be the Godfather.

Michael has passed the test, but you wouldn't have entered it, would you? No matter the anger you felt and the urge to avenge your father, would you have shot these two men in the forehead? Wouldn't you have reported them to the police? But one of them *is* the police. So the medium, its balance of action and removal, is your hired killer.

Well, you doubt you could have hit the two foreheads even at the range of a few feet. Firing a gun is not as sweet as the movies make it seem. But Michael had been a Marine—he surely learned to shoot; we expect that much of Marine training. Lee Harvey Oswald was nearly three years in the Marines, and while he was not in combat, he scored rankings as "sharpshooter" and "marksman" in his tests.

Whatever the restrictions or hesitations—would you have done it? Could you have shot accurately? I think there is no doubt about your, or our, willing participation in the movie event. We are decent people, aren't we? We are law-abiding by instinct, and pacific in temperament. If our ticket to the movie has an assigned seat, we sit there in obedience. Sometimes we get fired up by a screen situation, but we do not carry guns, do we? And we do not believe in violence, even as we give it our energy on screen? But we get a kick out of guns and movies, we have learned to do their murders with panache. Imagined firing can be an acquired habit.

A lot of people who frequent the movies are aware of having dull and disappointing lives, with some pain or unhappiness. Sitting in the dark they feel anonymous and insignificant. But is that why they go to the movies, or what the medium has done to them? Or us? It is a hard sad life, crushed by its realism. Sometimes a doctor can examine a "difficult" child and conclude: he has "a vivid fantasy life, turning around the topics of omnipotence and power, through which he tries to compensate for his present shortcomings and frustrations."

Quiz question: was that verdict handed down for Francis Coppola, Donald Trump, Stanley Kubrick, Jack Nicholson, John F. Kennedy, Lee Harvey Oswald, you, or me? Answer on p. 143.

Michael goes away after the killings—it was a double murder, in a regarded restaurant. There will be heat. Even if the Corleone-friendly media can expose police corruption and the Sollozzo involvement in narcotics, still the cops could have a grudge. So Michael goes to Sicily until the crisis wears off. And there he finds a hero's reward: Apollonia (Simonetta Stefanelli), a beautiful local girl. He marries her and there is a quick note of sexual splendor as she uncovers her breasts—this is more attention than Diane Keaton's Kay gets in three *Godfather* films. Not that Michael is really interested in talking to a woman. Apollonia has very little English, and then she's blown up in a car explosion that was meant for Michael. Vengeance is a currency and this one knows the map of Sicily by heart.

The restaurant execution (served before the veal) is in the heroic mythology, or an aria on omnipotence, that has always been indulged in movies. That opens up the question of whether *The Godfather* is concerned with killing or with murder. Is there that much difference? We do not really think to ask such questions in the aplomb and reputation of the films. It's not only that *The Godfather* won Oscars for Best Picture, for lead actor, and for screenplay. It had another eight nominations: for Caan, Robert Duvall, and Pacino as supporting actors; for direction, costumes, sound, editing, and music. To which I would only remark on the omission of Gordon Willis for cinematography and Dean Tavoularis for production design.

Beyond that, *The Godfather* had a worldwide gross of $245 million; in the interval between *The Sound of Music* and *Jaws*, it was the most lucrative film there had ever been. *The Godfather Part II* was to come. That won six Oscars (Best Picture, Robert De Niro as supporting actor, Coppola as director, screenplay, Dean Tavoularis for art direction, and music again). It had another five nominations (for Pacino, Michael V. Gazzo, and Lee Strasberg as supporting actor, Talia Shire as supporting actress, and costume). Still no Gordon Willis—some fix was in.

For many critics, *Part II* was a subtler and more expansive film, a sequel that enlarged the original, and enough to reassess those two parts as a single work. But *Part II* did less well at the box office. Was it difficult instead of smooth? Were the time shifts disconcerting? Were we getting bored with the same old thing?

Was the story really too chilling? Had we acquired some earnest disapproval of murder as a game, or did we secretly respond to the bleak confidence uttered by Michael in *Part II* that "we can kill anybody."

Just do it with style. At the close of the original film, Michael stands as godfather in the baptism of his sister Connie's child. The liturgy of that scene, which includes the renunciation of Satan and all his works, is intercut with scenes from the coup that Michael has ordered and directed in his business. In Las Vegas, the rebellious Moe Greene is getting a back rub. Stretched out on the table, he looks up as a stranger enters the parlor. He puts on his glasses and is shot dead through the right lens. There is an executioner's satisfaction in this—put on your spectacles so I have a target to aim at—that is beyond mere execution.

One Tattaglia brother is shot in an elevator; another meets gunfire in a locked revolving door. The engineering of everyday mechanisms is made sublime in the killings. Another man and his lover are shot to pieces in bed. It's likely that that woman had not offended, but she happens to be there, so she is gone.

Finally, the archvillain, Barzini (Richard Conte), has his fatal finale. He had expected to have a limo waiting outside his grand building. But some cop is ticketing it for parking (a sweet law-abiding touch), except that the cop is gangster Al Neri (Richard Bright), who shoots two Barzini henchmen and then takes out Barzini himself—a deft long shot with a handgun—so that Barzini can tumble down the fancy steps to his building.

Eight executions in a row, all gems delivered with magnificent brevity. Not one shabby or casual killing in the show. You want to stand up and cheer. You want to join the family?

Amid the enchantment of the first two parts of *The Godfather*, there were attempts to say the films were a critique of gangster attitudes, and of the corrupting force of business in America. I understand that impulse—and it came from Francis Coppola himself. It is a pretty thing to have huge success, prizes, and money, but don't forget the bonus of feeling respectable and ennobled.

This matter is too tricky, and the legacy is too far-reaching for complacency. It is a white lie to give *The Godfather* some seal of respectable approval, and that ignores the marriage of meticulous craft, a sheer talent for film, and the intellectual shallowness of murderous cinema. The enterprise cannot see or admit how far it has rounded us up in the militia named Corleone. Coppola did admit—as if with surprise—that the set got crowded whenever they were doing a shoot-out scene. Onlookers were hungry to see the tumbling bodies, the expertise of legend that takes out Moe Greene's eye.

Don't you shudder to think of a bullet being fired into your eye and then into the brain? Yes, its effect would be quick, but isn't that death hideous? Suppose you were the hired assassin, would you shoot Moe in the back—reliably dead—or would you actually muster the precise cruelty to shoot him in the eye? Do you see how such considerations are easily eclipsed by the "Wow!" of it all and the marvel of cinema where you get the thrill while knowing it's only a movie so you can let your own suppressed malice or violence run riot? Where's the actual damage, you say? Alex Rocco, the actor who played Moe Greene, lived on till 2015.

The movies have glamorized the life of the Mafia. Every careful report says their criminal activity is minor compared with the ceaseless exploitation by our major corporations and the political forces that are accomplice to them. If you want a crime film, filled with polite hourly violence, try *Margin Call*, where the only death is that of a dog.

It's not just that shooting out someone's eye is appalling, or that the Mafia is a minor part of what is wrong in America. It's that the membership of a militia like the Corleone family is one that none of us would want to admit to. So do we need the dark to gain entrance? Those thugs are ill-educated, brutish, boring, and ugly with women. Just note the forlorn place of Kay in the saga, a woeful face shut out of so many manly enclaves, an onlooker who has given up her innocence to suspend disbelief in her guy. She and women in general have no place in this culture—and America must rid itself of that constricting orthodoxy. In a really trenchant extension of *The Godfather*—one made by Luis Buñuel, say, or Robert Bresson—one might have Michael deciding to have Kay killed, because she knows too much and could one day testify against him.

As it is, in *Part II*, Michael has his brother Fredo killed, because Fredo is inept, a traitor, or too human. But now let Kay be his target. And suppose in some plot contrivance the task of killing her falls to Michael himself. Perhaps he takes this on out of loathing and a fear of women. Or has he always resented Kay as a silent, nagging reproach? He wants respect. Total respect, a fascist imperative.

Then say that murdering Kay goes badly; it lacks style or aplomb. He tries to strangle her, but he is not good at it. He uses a knife and makes a hash of that so there is blood everywhere—that sticky red mess—but still the task is not accomplished. He has no gun; he does not carry one, just as the British royal family has no money—and because its weight would spoil the line of his silk suit. So he has to beat her, with a statuette he was given for charitable works. This becomes the most extended and least polished murder in the Corleone franchise, and even dedicated fans sit there in appalled silence at its horror. The pretty face of Diane Keaton, as iconic as Doris Day was once, is so crushed—an eyeball has slid down her cheek—that it tests our faith in makeup. The film flops. It's like dog shit on your shoe.

CRUEL BEING KIND

My imagined addition to the *Godfather* series is meant to be upsetting. You'll never have to see that death of Kay, but how many times have you had to sit through similar movie spectacles— or worse? We saw Evelyn Mulwray's eye shot out at the end of *Chinatown* (1974). I wanted you to shudder, but that may betray my age. For I recollect a time when shuddering hadn't really started yet. People were just childishly afraid at the movies; they went there with some cozy danger in mind. You could watch Clouzot's *Diabolique* (1955) as a teenager, and wonder whether you were going to have a heart attack, just like the wife in the film. *Psycho* then was five years ahead. But our ancestors said they got their shivers from grave softies like Bela Lugosi in *Dracula* or Boris Karloff in *Frankenstein*, and it's unkind to belittle those fears. The history of being afraid is a current in which we are all trying to swim. Just ask yourself how demanding terror will be in ten years' time.

We think we know what cruelty means, but it is a shifty habit. An observer, watching some homeless on the city streets, was sure a pet dog was being mistreated. He reported the incident and soon that dog was taken away to safety. Its owner, indigent and derelict, was left on the streets at liberty but without his last solace.

It is a serious offense to beat your children; it requires public intervention if those children are not being fed or properly cared for. As if caring is defined in our Bill of Rights. But it is reckoned part of the everyday course of events if parents let their children be exposed to the steady beat of advertising in their media. Some cruelties take longer to cause damage. But some kindness takes responsibility for watchful severity. In *The Road*, the father makes sure the son understands the gun and the bullet that is there for the son to remove himself if the challenge of their predatory society comes too close. In Sussex, once the war began, Leonard and Virginia Woolf had cyanide tablets in case of invasion and occupation. Still, in a free country, Virginia filled her pockets with stones and walked into the Ouse River. This makes a very pretty, tragic image in *The Hours* as Nicole Kidman enters the dark cold water and the recurring Philip Glass music grinds with the passion of a water wheel or a tide.

Films in the heyday of the medium dealt in murder less often than is our habit now, and seldom in suicide, but the rules of conduct were more strict once. In *Laura* (1944), Diane Redfern is shot in the face (this allows the world to think that it is Laura Hunt who has been killed), but we do not have to see that ruined face. In *The Big Sleep* (1946), five supporting characters are murdered, but the suffering and destruction are smoothed over. No one dying howls for half an hour, or for another ten years. There's only one killing in *The Big Sleep* that hurts, the poisoning of Harry Jones (Elisha Cook), and that's a kind of honorable suicide. In the others, the victims clutch at their abdomens and topple over. It could be indigestion got them.

This was how kids came out of the movie theatre to play, firing finger six-guns at friends who then did extravagant death falls. It was such a lark. And it was like a careless sun shining on a swamp and not admitting that in 1944–46 new degrees of slaughter had been revealed at Auschwitz or Hiroshima. *The Best Years of Our Lives* was the prized movie of that moment, and it had an actor, Harold Russell, who had really lost his hands in the war. But not one death was shown in that film. Our newspaper photographs of concentration camps and atomic bomb casualties were carefully regulated so as not to be unduly distressing.

The fear or the horror seemed under control still. Even when unpleasant matters of murder were mentioned, the damage was kept distant. In *The Third Man* (1949), Holly Martins is made to grow up by being taken to see children in a hospital who have been ruined by Harry Lime's tainted penicillin, but we do not have to see those faces. When Lime himself dies, he nods consent at Holly, we hear a shot, and that's it. No need for Harry's guts spilling out in the Viennese sewer. No place for his screams echoing in the tunnels. Even so, in 1949 *The Third Man* was said to be uncommonly gritty and realistic.

If you're old enough to have a sense of what fear meant in 1945, then you have to admit that the broad sweep of film history has taken on a mounting stress that could leave your grandparents stunned, and even less inclined to have faith in life. Death has become an orthodoxy—and a commitment to imagined or dreaded states. It amounts to a state of religious being looking towards some dead end (or afterlife) to ignore our present liveliness in . . . life. Is that going too far? Is it too gloomy? I hope you're right.

In 1949, I was struck by the word "Kind" at the start of the title, but at eight I was not ready for the irony that lay behind it. *Kind Hearts and Coronets* was an unprecedented film over which people far wiser than eight were riveted by the eloquent insolence of Louis Mazzini. He was a wicked treat, and a new sort of screen person. He was a murderer devoted to language, who seemed to understand that self-pity was the worst faux pas a gentleman could make.

That taste for words was foundational, for Louis told the film's story. He was its master in a way that spelled out how vulnerable films were to mastery. Movie is a fascistic form, sort of, or one that enslaves viewers. Alfred Hitchcock used to say that his ambition—he said this in his droll, teasing way—was to put audiences through it, to abuse their devotion. It worked.

Kind Hearts had a similar tease in the soothing, articulate intelligence of the actor Dennis Price, who was not simply "well spoken" (in terms of elocution), but superior, amused, and literary. He spoke in sentences; and in the naturalism that has often oppressed cinema, formal grace can seem sinister or subversive. Price's Mazzini would sooner speak a beautiful sentence than endure a drab life sentence. So he is not daunted by the imminent hangman. Price and Mazzini alike are as assured as actors who know their parts: in 1902, Louis Mazzini is in Pentonville Prison, about to be hanged for murder. So he defies fate by writing his memoirs—language to the end.

Kind Hearts and Coronets was a comedy—nothing about the film was more challenging than that. But that creative decision was crucial. The film's writer-director, Robert Hamer, had just made two grim and lifelike movies about crime: in *Pink String and Sealing Wax*, Googie Withers plays a wife in Victorian Brighton who seeks to poison her intolerable husband; in *It Always Rains on Sunday*, Withers is a married woman with another unfeeling husband; she tries to shelter a lover who has escaped from prison. These are very good films centered on how unrewarding life can be. It is a trap.

Hamer was a trapped man, too. A brilliant, middle-class boy, he had been expelled from Cambridge. He became an alcoholic and he was homosexual, at a time when that way of being was illegal. Louis Mazzini has two women who love him, but he plays them off against each other in his own mind; it is the recourse of a masked gay personality. Louis is the poor relative of an aristocratic family, the D'Ascoynes. His mother, the child of the Duke of Chalfont, was infatuated with a moneyless Italian singer who died just as Louis was born. So Louis is an outcast: he lives not in Chalfont Castle but at 73 Balaclava Avenue in the gray suburbia of southwest London. He is poor and powerless, until he trusts language.

Thus he sets out to remove the eight members of the D'Ascoyne family who stand in the way of his becoming duke. The immediate claim to fame of the film was that Alec Guinness played all eight of these victims. He was admirable and inventive in his brief moments as the eight—eccentric, inane, and stupid, all of them, and so deserving of their fate. This film was made in 1949, in the midst of a Labour government whose chief aim was to have Britain survive the burden of victory in the war and to make the country decent (this was the government that introduced the National Health Service). The film is set in 1902, of course, in Edwardian England, but Louis is an upstart—his names are the essence of foreign threat, so his pruning of one aristocratic tree is a gesture towards a new order. His malice has a reformist thrust.

Not that Louis is preoccupied with any motivation. He wants the castle and the status it will bring. He wants his natural aristocracy recognized, but that is more mental acuity than a wish for nobility. In Price's screen presence and his voice there is a hint that he is bored and needs something to do. He has two women in his life, the upright Edith (Valerie Hobson) and the cunning and more naturally supine Sibella (Joan Greenwood). Having two avoids the narrow dedication of just one. It pushes Louis into the deceptions that suit his character. But we know just from listening to the women that Sibella is his true partner, because Joan Greenwood's drawled slyness is the female critique he deserves. Sometimes an opponent offers better company than a friend.

Michael Balcon, the head of Ealing Films, was reluctant to make the picture—he thought so many murders would repel an audience. But when Alec Guinness read the first script (which had only four murders), he wrote back, laughing, and demanded eight. He was correct: the film depends on its excess, for that turns the murders into movements in a dance or pearls on a string. You say murder should not be treated that way? It's in bad taste? You're right, but then wonder why the God-fearing Guinness wanted more. Do we admire that persistence? Or are you closer to sharing Michael Balcon's feeling that irony can go only so far?

A 106-minute movie isn't supposed to go further than being funny, provocative, and unsettling. As such, *Kind Hearts and Coronets* should be placed in the category of the acid comedies by Luis Buñuel—*That Obscure Object of Desire, Belle de Jour, The Criminal Life of Archibaldo de la Cruz* (truly a film about wanting to commit murder)—that see the chance of a mass medium in undermining fixed but bogus bourgeois points of view. Louis Mazzini is a rascal—he deserved to hang for it in 1902 (though we have largely given up that move in the game—except in the threatened United States). We know now that rascals with a unique way of speaking deserve to be on television talk shows, or the pretend politics shaped by such entertainments.

Seventy years later, *Kind Hearts* looks like a shining light, and one of those comedies that had seriousness in its heart. Just because we're laughing need not mean we're stupid. But in America, in 1949, the film shocked enough to be cut by six minutes with a different ending that ensured justice would rebuke Louis. (The English original ends on one of the sublime hesitations in cinema—I'll leave you to find it for yourself.)

It is a film a child could see—I was taken to it by a grandmother who never killed anyone, except in small talk. The murders are as pretty and amusing as surprise gifts. There is no malice in them and no disfiguring, let alone blood, pain, or torment. Of course, it's often the case that real murders (such as Reg Christie was pursuing at the same moment) could be so horrible in the showing as to be impossible. Louis Mazzini is a figure in our heritage (and not only Britain's), and he can be placed in a tradition that includes Oscar Wilde and Vladimir Nabokov (his *Pale Fire* is one of the most exquisite murder mysteries).

But the part of me that has lived another seventy years after being eight sees our changed ways. If I were in a position to mount a double bill for you, bizarre but fertile, I would pair *Kind Hearts and Coronets* with David Fincher's *Seven* (1995), or *Se7en*, a remarkably misanthropic film, even if its grim humor is subdued by the valiant yet hopeless American wish for law and order. I admit, the matching is not perfect: eight murders there and only seven here. Never mind: compromise is necessary sometimes.

Seven is as ghastly as it is revelatory. I like to think a lot of you could walk out of it—and did so—in indignation or dismay. An author likes to feel he has decent readers.

Just as our intimacy with Louis guides *Kind Hearts*, so *Seven* seems based on the partnership of its two detectives. This could be a hopeful deal: the brash rookie white guy Mills (Brad Pitt) and the wiser black veteran Somerset (Morgan Freeman), who is poised to retire. They operate in a pitiless city where a rain seems to fall most of the time, a rain like scum. The city is not named in the movie, though its locations were in and around Los Angeles. Mills has a new wife (Gwyneth Paltrow), and Somerset is drawn into their orbit out of kindness and sympathy—and his loneliness. These are the cops we like to imagine for ourselves: honest, resolute, humane.

But being humane is under threat. As the film begins, the two cops are assigned to what will be a serial killer at work in their city. He is a rare operator. He has the warped intellectual meticulousness that mixes Sherlock Holmes or a designer of chess puzzles with star torturers from the pit of Auschwitz. As a task, or an experiment, he is bent on seven murders to illustrate the seven deadly sins, and his cruel genius in devising them leaves arty clues for the detectives. (Did he foresee these two pursuers in advance? He leaves nothing to chance.) You can say he is a "real-life killer." But isn't he more an actor who wants his movie?

The story of *Seven* (written by Andrew Kevin Walker) is driven by this killer, and he is all the more significant—or alluring, or glamorous?—because he is withheld from view for some time. If that seems counterintuitive, just think how Harry Lime is awaited in *The Third Man*, or how dominant Hannibal Lecter is in *The Silence of the Lambs* on a mere twenty minutes of screen time. But that is how David Fincher has organized his film.

Fincher is one of the few exceptional and personal directors left in America. When I say personal I am talking not just about the authentic signature of his style—he is a planner more than a poet, and an expert with the camera, with sound and actors—but in his choice of material. He is a killer—or he cannot restrain his attraction to that urge. He killed off Sigourney Weaver's Ripley in *Alien 3*. He is also the director of *The Game*, *Fight Club*, *Panic Room*, *Zodiac*, *The Curious Case of Benjamin Button*, *The Social Network*, *The Girl with the Dragon Tattoo*, and *Gone Girl*. He is a key creator of *Mindhunter* for Netflix.

Only one of those films lacked his suave, dismissive authority, and that was *Benjamin Button*, his attempt to be drawn to common humanity (and his least coherent work). For the rest, he studies physical violence and its ecstatic nihilism (*Fight Club*), the paranoia of being pursued by killers (*Panic Room*), the intellectual charm of plotting (*The Game*), the suppressed malice or indifference to others in people of high intelligence (*The Social Network*), and the savage spectacle of damage (*The Girl with the Dragon Tattoo* and *Gone Girl*). Or, quite simply, our chronic fascination with murder in *Zodiac*. If you had a son who did those pictures one after the other, you might think of whispering to the police about him.

That leaves *Seven*, a film in which Fincher suggests that he wants to believe in the police. If you have walked out of it, or considered that self-protection, you know what I mean about its calm delight in the grotesque assault on human beings and their flesh. And the contempt it has for actual police intelligence. Equally, Hannibal Lecter is always a step ahead of the Starlings and Will Grahams pursuing him. *Seven* is a series of hysterically inventive murders in which the aura of cruelty cannot be distinguished from the calculation of the killer and the way the film is accomplice to that murderous superiority. The detectives voice our horror at what they are finding, but nothing stops the alliance of director and killer and the self-satisfaction in the execution. Fincher is clearly a son of *Psycho* (made two years before he was born) in trusting movie's capacity for outrage and our reluctance to tell it to go to hell.

The details are unrelentingly graphic: to demonstrate gluttony a man has been forced to eat until his stomach bursts—here are the spilled guts; for greed a pound of flesh has been taken from a lawyer's body, with detrimental effects; for sloth, a drug dealer has been chained to his bed and left to rot; a whore is raped and killed to warn of lust. That's four. And there are three more to come. The last two reach Mills where he lives and compel him to be a murderer in the name of wrath.

I am in awe of much of what Fincher has done—though it dismayed me at first, *Zodiac* is an exceptional and original film aware of the culture of morbidity in the news. But I flinch from the climate of his work, and remind myself of another weather system that includes Bresson, Buñuel, Bergman, Ophuls, Ozu,

Renoir, Mizoguchi, and so many others. I could bear the thought that Fincher had never existed. I cannot see that the bulk of his work does not encourage murder and cruelty (or our helplessness with it), and it hurts me as a film person, a movie man, to think that that is what excelling in cinema has come to.

That's where the nature of the killer in *Seven* is so challenging. His presence, his identity, and his appearance are gradually revealed as the film progresses. He is called John Doe, as if he were one of us, and he is played by Kevin Spacey.

When Spacey was cast as John Doe it seemed a sensible decision. He was just winning his supporting actor Oscar for Keyser Söze in *The Usual Suspects*, a demure and effacing master-murderer in a teasing film. He was an exceptional actor, and in saying that I think of his Mel Profitt in the TV series *Wiseguy* (1987–90), such films as *L.A. Confidential* and *American Beauty* (where he won a full Oscar), and his Hickey in a London production of *The Iceman Cometh*. He has made his share of bad or foolish pictures, not least *Beyond the Sea*, in which his Bobby Darin was a bold and demented labor of love. But Spacey is the real and lasting thing: insightful, risk-taking, and ambiguous.

He may not be a pleasant person—but being fairly familiar with film history and having met a number of actors, I am not taken aback by that. Spacey often seemed tricky or untrustworthy—a type of screen personality that has included Cary Grant, Margaret Sullavan, Robert Mitchum, Jeanne Moreau, Dirk Bogarde, and so many actors I cherish. I can believe he behaved badly sometimes and forced himself sexually upon others in his business and his art. But I feel inclined to adopt a Captain Renault–like stance with such news. The unpleasant man in Spacey did also save the Old Vic theatre in London.

I disliked the way he was deleted from *All the Money in the World* (2017) just because his personal reputation had been discredited. I would note that the several companies for whom he made and makes money and glory have not withdrawn his films: one can still rent *The Usual Suspects* or *American Beauty*. Netflix is still streaming *House of Cards* (on which it made a fortune and a foundation for its empire), even as it canceled the show after six seasons, and Spacey after five. Kevin Spacey may never make another film; he may be dead to his art—and that will be a loss to all of us as well as to the other people who could be employed on his projects.

All that said, I cannot think of other actors who would have made me detest *Seven* so much. Pitt and Freeman are both likable in the film, but it is clear that they are waiting for their Godot to arrive. When he comes, Spacey is gloating, masterly, delicately comic and toxic, and wearing evil as a perfume. But in being all that he raises and then surpasses the habitual questions: Are killers crazy? Or is there any use in facing that challenge? I am coming to that in a more considered way, but for the moment I will just say that Spacey's Doe and Anthony Hopkins's Hannibal Lecter are beyond rebuke or forgiveness. We are watching actors, or characters, who have resolved to get through life by acting. This is deeply disturbing, and I do see how Fincher might say, "Look, I am depicting the end of the world, of integrity and life itself. Aren't I doing it well?"

Yes, he is. That is a regular problem with movie outrage; its spectacle can be so enticing—and misleading—for those in the safe dark. We should not shut ourselves off from the historical perspective. My grandmother taking me to see *The Third Man* was thrilled at its dangers, but she might have dropped dead on encountering *Seven*. Outrageous ideas can kill us as reliably as guns and knives. 1949 to 1995 was less than fifty years. And in another fifty, imagine the movies that could be on offer then. Will they involve the instructional rape and murder of infants? Will our present notions of pain and damage have become sentimental? Will movies have crossed over the line and made a deal that allows them to kill actors, on camera, in our plain sight? Will we sit there for that? Just because we feel alone? Cut off.

A LARK! AN ASIDE

I hope you can handle this gravity—so long as it does not topple into solemnity. But I have to say this: the folks doing these movie killings are having a grand time. So much so, they can hardly stop laughing. If you look closely, that corpse over there—the third one to the left, the one with the hole in his head—isn't he simmering with suppressed giggles at all this pretending?

Long ago, when pretending was all the rage, kids studied shoot-out scenes in Westerns to see whether some villain could actually stop breathing in his death shot. Actors and crews knew that fun, just as they were tickled when blood sachets and electrical discharges came into use so bad guys could become a pretty light show of damage and destruction. Of course, by now, CGI can handle all those things, so there isn't the same glee on set when lavish death scenes come into play, and strangers gather just to watch.

"We had to take Jake's death scene twenty-seven times!" you hear the story. "He was a nervous wreck! But the laughter and the jokes? It was such a merry day."

I made that up, but it's not an exaggeration. And just as an aside, I do think it's worth noting the disconnect between what's being depicted and the ingenious hilarity in doing it. There are movie craftsmen who come home for dinner and family after a long day in which they disposed of several thousand stick figures with that wholesome feeling of weariness.

ARE MURDERERS CRAZY?

Is John Doe mad in *Seven*? Or just brilliant and lonely, a light in his own dark? Does it help to pin these labels on him? Once upon a time, we were told there could be a pitch of evil in mankind that was simply insane. Over the edge. This was how Hitler was explained to me when I was a child, and it was said with a sigh of relief, as if, Thank God, his monstrousness had been dealt with so we could all move on. But have we ever reconciled ourselves to what he and his people did? These days, is anyone exactly deranged in movies if we are paying to watch? Doesn't commodification act like Valium?

In *Seven*, John (can I call him that?) is one of the most organized and authoritative people in cinema. He plans and devises murders that would be beyond the imagining of most of us, and which are too concerned with carnal disintegration to entertain Agatha Christie. You'd have to love your work to have such care and patience over it. And John does seem highly intelligent—or is it inordinately so, as if to say too much intelligence can drive you crazy? Do we cling to that warning? As if to say, truly, or ideally, we are sentient beings, full of feeling. Or could it be that excessive feeling makes us more disturbed? As it is, when John wants to get Mills and Somerset out to that last yellowing location, not quite desert but desolate (it was near Lancaster, northeast of Los Angeles), where only Federal Express would go, he tells them that if they don't go along with his plan, he'll plead insanity when his trial comes up. Can anyone able to make an insanity plea a pawn in his game really be insane?

In John's defense (and it would be no surprise if he chose to be his own lawyer), you could say that he has a purpose in life; he sees practical problems and solves them; he seems to be in possession of enough money to follow his hobby, and having money is often a way of reappraising madness as eccentricity; he speaks clearly, with point and effect; he can hold opposed ideas in his mind—thus he is cruel but amused by it all. Above all, he does seem to pass in life, to get along—his apartment may be a shambles (like a furious author's room, like the book-packed home of Doktor Peter Kien, in Elias Canetti's *Auto-da-Fé*), but he lives there without upsetting his neighbors. Also, he stimulates opposed attitudes in us: we abhor John Doe, but we would like him to have more scenes.

Something devious and very telling has occurred in the presented self of the unkind mastermind. Once upon a time, murder mysteries, or detective stories, hinged on the exceptional intelligence of the detective. But a secret rapport developed between the acuity of a Holmes and the plotting ingenuity of his maker. One cannot say that Hannibal Lecter's author, Thomas Harris, disapproved of him. That monster made Harris's fortune and displayed his cleverness. That is why I suggest that John Doe is not just the master of *Seven*, but virtually its author. Greater works have grown out of this principle: for example, Nabokov's *Pale Fire* (1962), in which a supposedly hideous and deplorable killing is also the enactment of an intricate self-loving plot. Nabokov threw off that aside about murderers and their fancy prose style. But it is an insightful accusation.

Nabokov presided over *Pale Fire* and his later works with the self-satisfied aplomb of a gentleman at ease in the Montreux Palace Hotel. He lived there with his handsome and obedient wife, Vera, writing out formal answers for interviewers, inventing chess problems, thinking of butterflies, and composing his books on index cards, knowing they would be great. That assurance is his fanciness. As interesting, but less composed, is the Bret Easton Ellis who wrote *American Psycho* (1991) about a Wall Street investment banker who turns to serial killing. Ellis admitted to the alienation and isolation that prompted his book: "I was slipping into a consumerist kind of void that was supposed to give me confidence and make me feel good about myself but just made me feel worse and worse and worse about myself." The fancy style and the elegant regard for murder can come out of rapt self-loathing.

You're going to say this is perverse special pleading for John

Doe or looking on the bright side. The ironies abound, and they can make you cynical, but in our world it's not unreasonable to think that some Hollywood people might approach a John Doe in real life and ask—innocent or guilty—could we film your story? I suspect John would be charmed (and not for the money—he wants it done for its own sake), and he would have only one proviso: *he has to play the part himself.* Which only leads us to how he has been acting out all along.

Is Norman Bates insane? Can an actor play a madman without making his chaos emblematic? Doesn't Norman know he's going to be "a type"?

At first in *Psycho*, it's Janet Leigh doing the "crazy" things, thinking she can get away with $40,000. So when her desperate drive north comes to rest, there is Norman to give her a room for the night and a simple cold supper. He is the gentlest, kindest, most discerning person in the film so far—and *Psycho* acquires resonance in the lengthy conversation he and Marion share. This is the man, sitting in his chair, his eloquent hands shaping the air, who says to Marion when she mentions the "private traps" in which people live,

> And none of us can ever get out. We—we scratch and claw, but—only at the air—only at each other. And for all of it, we never budge an inch.

There it is, hanging in the night air like a northern Californian chill—the most heartfelt and aware line in the film, and as philosophical or revelatory as Hitchcock ever allowed himself in forty years. This is a troubled man, but is he mad? Or just lonely? Marion, for one, is touched by him. And Norman feels that.

There are some disturbing cracks in this gentle Norman: he gets angry over the idea of difficult people being shut away; there is an odd affinity between him and the stuffed birds on the wall. He's a lonesome kid; that's why Anthony Perkins was such good casting. There is rapport: Marion is troubled that this fierce mother dominates him with her echoing voice. And he is touched by her. It is when Norman is aroused by Marion (just like us) that Mother rears up with her big sharp knife.

There is even a movielike prospect as Marion retires for the night that the two of them might make a bond next morning. I know, she's having her affair with Sam, but he's not very interesting or perceptive, whereas Norman's wide eyes and Perkins's tender smile understand pathos and loss. He is full of feeling, and his loneliness needs rescuing. Marion and Norman might not seem that promising a couple, but the hint is there. Imagine a story with those two, settling down, with Mother watching from a distance and Norman telling her, "Don't you say one word!"

In truth, granted the intense pressure in its first forty minutes, I wonder if *Psycho* doesn't go to hell afterwards. There is the Arbogast murder, a tour de force of mise en scène and moving camera, as if Hitchcock needed to show that he could kill that way too. But the unfolding of the mystery is long-winded and anticlimactic. The eventual psychological explanation is a cockamamie tidying up. It is said that Hitch embraced the actor playing the shrink (Simon Oakland) and told him he'd saved the picture. That's an admission from the director that the show risked being preposterous. Perhaps Hitch lost some interest after the shower, and dreaded the need for a Poirot-like explanation on how Norman and Mother were battling elements in one mind—allowing the grand guignol of that last scene where Mother stares out at us, looking like Norman, but speaking in a woman's voice until the face dissolves into the skull and the swamp.

So we are meant to believe that Norman really was insane? And that startles us? What rankles or disappoints in that is that many of us have two (or more) competing voices in our head—that is what makes Norman so complex and appealing in the supper scene. He is in flux, just like Marion, the good girl who went over the edge. *Psycho* finishes on a sort of flourish, but think how powerful it could have been had Norman come in for cross examination (after he'd showered and discarded Mother's clothes), and seemed like the old Norman again but with Mom pushing her way into him, putting words and gender intonation into his mouth. That comes close to John Doe in *Seven*, a disconcerting mixture of the ladylike and the monstrous.

A murderer in real life should be appalling, not just to his victims but to the people who knew him and realized the story too late. Reginald Christie was mean-faced (it's the only way to say it—if he's your dentist you're not going), but people found him withdrawn, rather dull, low-level nasty, until the truth was revealed. Whereupon it was possible to reinterpret Christie as a furtive English malignance quietly getting away with it all for years. In the era of Christie I had a father who matched part of that description, not that he killed anything except hope in a few people who found themselves close to him. But when Richard Attenborough played Christie—he said he had never felt so involved in a part—he abandoned the ordinary inscrutability of Christie. That film became a portrait of an actor hiding from the world. Because actors don't like inscrutability.

It is the ordinariness of murder that is hard to convey in films, what Hannah Arendt called the banality of evil. For decades now, there has been a helpless, passive readiness for taking on murderers as the protagonists in bloody franchises. Such films are often numbered, as if to admit they have no originality. Here is the boredom and banality of murder aligned with the automatic invocation of psychosis. The origin of that tendency is one of the most influential films ever made—Fritz Lang's *M* (1931).

I mentioned Lang earlier as an influence on Hitchcock. The German director loved crime stories and he had a master criminal of his own, Dr. Mabuse, who pretended to be raving mad. He was seen in *Dr. Mabuse the Gambler* (1922) and *The Testament of Dr. Mabuse* (1933), paranoid raptures on conspiracy in which the magician-like Mabuse wants control of the world so that he can destroy it. As played by Rudolf Klein-Rogge, Mabuse was omniscient, deranged but out of reach. He had no humanity; he was a ringmaster or a director who had lost control. *M* introduced a markedly different killer, a wistful lost soul who craved understanding.

The Mabuse films are crammed panoramas of urban frenzy,

and Lang liked to work on that large scale: he made two movies from Wagner's *Die Nibelungen*, as well as *Woman in the Moon*, an early science fiction picture. He did not naturally think to explore psychological personality. That changed with *M*. With his wife and screenwriter, Thea von Harbou, he was fascinated by a wave of serial killers who had alarmed the German public in the years after the Great War.

He was especially intrigued by Peter Kürten of Düsseldorf, a man who pursued small girls, raped them, and then strangled them. Sometimes he ejaculated as he heard the victim's last breath. He was captured, tried, and guillotined, in 1931, despite pleas of insanity, as Lang went into production on *M*. Kürten had planned his murders, and he was graphic about the gratification he had achieved with them. He murdered for pleasure— and maybe we should ask, is pleasure ever irrational? As he was executed, he asked the guillotine master whether he might still have enough hearing for an instant after decapitation and get the thrill of hearing blood and air rush out of his own body. Is that mad or just obsessive about getting the best out of every second? Or is that question intolerable? Isn't it part of intelligence that in its advance it creates questions that drive us out of order?

Lang had another reason for doing the film. In the late twenties, he had been impressed by a young actor on stage, Peter Lorre (born László Löwenstein in Hungary in 1903). Lorre was five-foot-three, not handsome, though his baby face attracted many photographers. He was an inspired, poetic actor drawn to experimental theatre as much as to the classics. When Lang saw him, he asked Lorre whether he had ever made a film. No, the actor replied. Then wait until I call for you, Lang instructed. In due course, he saw that Lorre would be perfect as the killer in *M*, named Hans Beckert, a strangler of children, though without Kürten's sexual habits. Lang never showed Beckert murdering any child: he left that to our imagination. Kürten's ejaculating on a dying body would be a tough test even today. Though we're becoming stoic over such things.

Lorre played the part, in a shroudlike overcoat and fedora. He looked like a desperate boy, and with sound his rare whining voice came to life. No doubt Lorre exaggerated this later because he knew people recognized it and heard a kind of invalid pathos. Through his own instinct and at Lang's direction he played the killer as a victim, whose body harbored murderousness along with blood and electrical neuronal discharges. There was something primitive in the look of Lorre, as raw as cell life, and he is the first screen presence to suggest that murderousness might be biological.

Beckert drifts through the city, soft, immature, and plaintive. It's as if he seeks out children for company, as well as for his base longings. But just because Lang can't show us the worst acts, so Lorre gathers pity and self-pity to himself. It's not his fault, it's a defect or an aptitude in cinema.

Lang makes a societal diagram out of *M*, and his city is the layout for a pitiless theorem. It has stage light instead of daylight. The air feels organized. So the police and the underworld imitate each other. They cannot endure the killer being in their city because regular business has been obstructed. So both law and outlawry hunt the killer. He resembles an alien or an artist figure, at odds with his world. Add that to Lorre's childlike image, and we begin to feel for this terrible man.

As he is hunted, there is a piercing moment when he realizes that a blind beggar, a part of the underworld, has planted a white chalk "M" on his dark coat to alert the city. He sees the letter over his shoulder in a mirror: it is the M in REDRUM.

Beckert is captured by the criminal organization, and we cannot help but feel some sympathy for him. A mock trial is staged in a factory cellar. It's then he has his say, and Lorre rises to the height of his emotional performance. He is a terrified wreck, in dread of the trial but still most horrified at himself. He is incoherent—but he is an actor doing incoherence. And we get caught up in his breathless spell:

> Always . . . always, there's this evil force inside me. . . . It's there all the time, driving me out to wander through the streets . . . following me . . . silently, but I can feel it there. . . . It's me, pursuing myself. . . . I want to escape . . . to escape from myself! . . . But it's impossible. I can't. I can't escape. I have to obey it, I have to run . . . run . . . streets . . . endless streets. I want to escape. I want to get away. I am pursued by ghosts. Ghosts of mothers. And of those children. They never leave me. . . . They are there always . . . except when I do it. . . . Then I can't remember anything. . . . And afterwards I see those posters and I realize. . . . Did I do that? But I can't remember anything about it . . .

The aria goes on; it is magnificent and often quoted; it is memorable—but it is a declaration of a crucial absence of memory.

I do not mean to eliminate or deride the helplessness or lost control some mentally disturbed people may feel. I know that some wander the streets talking to invisible companions and enemies, or kicking endlessly at stones on the ground that I cannot see. They rant at silence or sing to strangers, because they have lost their mind, or the mind has lost them. I see them in San Francisco, though sometimes they are regular people arguing with their earbud phones. They are in the kind of trap Norman Bates knows—which many have felt out there in the night. But Norman and Beckert are lonely talkers, and it is a tragedy of real madness that its victims have lost access to eloquence because they are not listened to.

Not the least of the ironies attached to *M* is that Peter Lorre felt "killed" by it as an actor. He was as talented as he was creatively ambitious. One may argue that his size, his shape, and his bulging eyes would always keep him from roles that an Olivier or a Spacey took on. But Lorre wished for the acting heights. And his very success in *M* and its acclaim for the rest of his life in the picture business—above all in America—had him cast perpetually as a killer, a madman, or a comic weirdo. He was told he should be "like Peter Lorre," an absurd demand but one that Hans Beckert would have understood.

SINGLE-HANDED

Because Beckert in *M* is such a killer, and a pent-up outburst waiting to break, it is easy to miss the core of his sensibility: he is alone, in a world in which it is so hard to make allegedly normal contact. He is held in place as much by guilt as by the mania that drives him. Looking at the world through the sights of a firearm or a plan to kill can be a way of defying isolation or armoring it against doubt.

> Slowly the sights came into line. Through the U of the back-sight could be seen a tiny triangle of white—the white of the jumper of the man on the bo'sun's chair. Up into the U crept the wedge of the foresight; it moved steadily upward until its tip was exactly in line with the top of the U. There it stayed for a tiny instant of time, the while Brown, mindful of his musketry training at Harwich, and his periodical practices since, steadied his breathing, took the first pull of the trigger, and slowly squeezed the trigger back further through the final

tenth of an inch. Then the rifle went off and the echo of its
report ran menacingly round the circle of the cliffs.

Brown is Leading Seaman Albert Brown, and the year is 1915. He
is about to become an efficient, cold-blooded killer, and our guy.

As part of the Great War and the service he has never ques-
tioned, Brown is a crew member on the cruiser *Charybdis*. Somewhere in the Pacific, the *Charybdis* engages the prized German
battleship *Ziethen*. The British ship is destroyed, but it has damaged the *Ziethen*. Brown has been rescued in the loss of his ship
and he is held as a prisoner on the *Ziethen*. He is well treated—
these Germans are not hateful beasts. But the German ship needs
repairs and so its captain seeks temporary refuge at the island
of Resolution, a speck in the sea in the Galápagos group. While
the *Ziethen* is docked there, with its great guns disabled, Brown
escapes with just a rifle and some ammunition. He clambers up
the sharp-edged lava slopes of the island and finds a cleft where
he can mount himself as a sniper. Then, as the German repair
crew starts to work, Seaman Brown begins to pick them off with
his rifle.

This is *Brown on Resolution*, by C. S. Forester, published in
1929. I found the novel when I was twelve because I had enjoyed
several of the Hornblower novels by Forester, an enthusiasm
prompted by the film *Captain Horatio Hornblower* (1951), in which
Gregory Peck played the English captain. But I was keen to read
Brown because Forester had once been a boy at my school, Dulwich College. So there was an odd call of duty in getting hold of

the book. But duty was soon buried in a pleasure that was more than spectatorship. I entered the story in spirit and imagination. I wanted to be Brown. So young at Dulwich, so intimidated by the school and by other frightening aspects of life, I needed a fantasy of being powerful. This is not so uncommon. Young men can fear life while being told that fear is unmanly. I would pull Brown's trigger.

Brown on Resolution was my first immersion in a grown-up book, and I was excited by the participation in reading and even writing. It felt like a going out into the world and making some contact with an esteemed author. But the book and the experience also defined loneliness and let me know it was mine, without regret or self-pity. I was a Brown, and resolved or identified in that casting. There is no real island of Resolution in the Pacific, but Forester had created the name in full understanding of what a youth needed.

Brown is a bastard child, the result of a passionate fling between Agatha Brown, a decent middle-class woman, daughter to a greengrocer in the London suburb of Lewisham, and Lieutenant-Commander Richard Saville-Samarez of the Royal Navy. They meet on a train—call it a brief encounter—and they fall into each other. He moves on in his career unaware that Agatha is pregnant. She has her son, Albert, and raises him properly in the line of duty. Albert Brown is headed for the navy, and his destiny coincides with the Great War.

This story now becomes more autobiography than literary

criticism, but at twelve—and maybe much later—we hardly know how to absorb a story without seeing it as our own. That is part of the attempt against loneliness in reading and writing. I liked *Brown on Resolution* because of Agatha; she is a more explored character than Albert. She does not complain about her situation, or about being left. She never imagines she could be an upper-class Mrs. Saville-Samarez. But she is a resolute mother who raises her boy without doubt or pomp.

I saw my own mother in that, for she had been left by my father when I was born. I don't know whether she loved him, but she must have tried when they first came together, because my mother was not dishonest or less than dutiful. She was to some intents a single mother, though my father came back every other weekend to maintain control of our house. He was a vital part of my life until about the time I read *Brown*. He taught me sports, and that was what we had to talk about. He came and went and in that rhythm he was there but he was not there. My solitude was defined and it found itself in reading and going to the movies, those immense glories in being alone.

So it was that Seaman Brown was a waiting vacant shape for me to enter: a humble boy, a bastard, but ready to play a part—significant yet unnoticed—in the war. Albert Brown's sniping delays the *Ziethen* long enough for it to fall victim to an English naval squadron in which Captain Saville-Samarez plays a leading part. There they were in the same theatre of action, father and son, unaware of each other's nearness or of the way their paths had crossed in the dark and their narrative had been completed. Only we know what happened.

I have never held a rifle; I doubt I ever will. But I grasp something of its appeal for people who feel their loneliness with the sensitivity that Seaman Brown works the trigger. I read *Brown on Resolution* over and over again because I was finding myself in the situation of this young man amid those sharp rocks, certain of his own death sooner or later, but picking off those white German figures as if they were pieces of fluff on his uniform.

There is an affinity that covers writing, reading, watching a film, and being a lone killer that is endlessly intriguing. *The Day of the Jackal* (1973) is an entertaining if shallow film, and I am not suggesting that the free world wanted Charles de Gaulle dead (though some contemporary politicians might have thought of it). But Fred Zinnemann's film from the Frederick Forsyth novel is beguiling. Much of that has to do with the affable, civilized, and rather gentle Edward Fox playing the Jackal. There was pressure on Zinnemann to cast a bigger name. Just think of Robert Shaw in the part, or Sean Connery, and their abrasive edge would change the film's tone. But the drawn-out process of preparation for the killing makes us hushed accomplices to it all, and Fox seems like a good fellow dedicated to his task. A part of me sees that film repeatedly in the daft hope that the Jackal might succeed—it is *his* day.

In the book and the film, the Jackal is hired as an assassin for $500,000, but the film is uninterested in the mercenary arrangement. Fox's killer is an artist almost, or a missionary, intent on the killing for its own sake, or as a puzzle to be solved. So when he makes his gun, that is a proof of his inventiveness and concentration.

There are two films from the Forester novel. The first, *Brown on Resolution*, was made in 1935, directed by Walter Forde, with the young John Mills as Brown. It is superior to the second film, *Sailor of the King* (also known as *Single-Handed*), directed by an Englishman, Roy Boulting, but with the American Jeffrey Hunter as Brown (the film says he is Canadian). Both films have the requisite moments of Brown aiming his gun and firing, then the fall of German sailors. But neither comes close to the gratification I felt with the novel. Still, the films, like the book, let an idea germinate: that there is a charm in solitude or loneliness and its satisfaction at insignificance being able to pick off some white figures in the distance. You could call them enemies in a just war, but a hundred years later justice in that Great War seems like a bleak joke. Forester goes so far as to imagine Brown's first target as a man named Zimmer from Hamburg, who has a pretty young blonde wife. "Then something hit him hard on the left side close to his heart, and for an instant of time he knew pain, agonizing pain, before darkness shut in upon him."

I have admitted that Forester was a tidy writer. It's so much more comfortable that Zimmer dies instantly, instead of hanging in his bosun's chair for hours in the sun, moaning interminably. But it has been a movie convention that deaths should occur in the clean snap of your fingers. Though in *Full Metal Jacket*, the Americans shot by the sniper in open ground do cry out in unrelieved pain so that other soldiers are driven to attempt rescue. Whereupon the sniper picks them off, too. Though she's just a girl, that sharpshooter is the enemy, the Vietcong, doing her duty. So something in us relishes her death—and Kubrick satisfies that urge. But isn't there also something that is with her? There are shots from her point of view with us looking through the sights of her gun. That attraction is rife with suggestion—it's so close to the operation of filming itself, of shooting, and the imperative of seeing at the movies. In being there, we have to look; and in looking through the sights, don't we have to shoot?

The mixed meanings in the word "shoot" are potent. As long ago as *Blow-Up* (1966), Michelangelo Antonioni presented Thomas (David Hemmings), whose nature as a human has been subsumed in his vocation, photography. He goes to an attractive and nearly deserted London park and starts snapping. Then he sees a couple in the distance kissing yet arguing. He photographs them. The woman (Vanessa Redgrave) sees this is happening. She approaches the photographer in anger. Her privacy has been stolen. She demands the roll of film. He teases her, and then much later his curiosity discovers the story line of a murder in these casual snaps. As he prints and enlarges pictures and puts them up on his wall in sequence, he feels the dual meaning of "shooting." We cannot avoid the predatory violence in shooting film. We like to think we are honest and honorable, but when we look, we are determined to see some buried story.

A camera lens and a telescopic sight are ways of finding meaning and targets; but their selectivity has a moral aspect. Clint Eastwood's *American Sniper* (2014) is derived from the military career of Chris Kyle, a sharpshooter who had more than 250 kills in four tours of Iraq. Bradley Cooper plays Kyle as an expert marksman who becomes disconcerted by his own prowess. He has to pick off a woman and a child who may be carrying a grenade. It is a civilian war in which uniform is no protection against doubt. Kyle kills a key terrorist with a shot of more than 2,000 yards. Eastwood makes this coup exciting, but distance does not always bring detachment when murder or military killing (if you are sure of the difference) is increasingly possible at remote distances. The farther away the enemy, the more theoretical he or she becomes. *American Sniper* was the box office hit of the year in a country eager to wash its hands of Iraq.

There was a film called *Suddenly*, made in 1954, that opened up a similar ambivalence. It's an effective melodrama at 77 minutes in which a would-be assassin takes over a house overlooking the railroad station in a small Californian town named Suddenly (the exteriors were shot in Saugus, a neighborhood of Santa Clarita). A train carrying the president is supposed to stop in Suddenly, and the assassin means to murder him. So he sets up in the hijacked house with a telescopic rifle mounted on a table.

The film exists for Frank Sinatra's rancid vitality as the assassin. At that point, Sinatra was on the upswing: he had won an Oscar in *From Here to Eternity* and he was launched on the long-playing albums that established him as a middle-aged romantic singer. He was immensely popular, and a part of him was eager to be liked. But there was a darker side to Sinatra—he could be ugly and spiteful in his behavior. And so he took the part of John Baron, the would-be killer, and played it to the hilt. He snarls and sneers; he is nasty as a character attempting an unthinkable crime for 1954. But he was still Sinatra, and that put a curious tremor in the film's suspense, akin to the secret way in which we want to see Marion Crane suffer in *Psycho*. Directed appropriately by Lewis Allen, *Suddenly* is not a deep picture: it has no intention of being that. But it is more unsettling than it knows, and it lingers in the imagination.

John Baron is not reflective so much as intensely expressive about killing. A few years later, Sinatra produced and acted in a better film, *The Manchurian Candidate*, in which an attempt is made to assassinate a presidential candidate. No one suggested that Sinatra was pursuing an idea or a narrative theme. He lacked the patience for that. But he was taken aback on November 22, 1963, when America suffered its most infamous and damaging lone gunman. Whether he was alone is one of the riddles in our paranoia. (And Oswald is the answer to page 101.)

Lee Harvey Oswald had done it all on his own—that was the first anguished story. He had gone to the sixth floor of the Texas School Book Depository where he worked, in Dallas, and he had shot the president in his motorcade. It was said straightaway that America produced these wayward guys and then let them have guns. So it had happened in broad daylight. What emerged about Oswald's biography suggested that he was disturbed, a loner, trying to emerge from American anonymity and his own fear of failure.

In 1988, Don DeLillo published a novel, *Libra*, that is an imagined investigation of Oswald. In his teens, for a couple of years Lee had lived in New York, and DeLillo depicts him riding the subway, without destination, but in rapport with its force and its infinite unknown crowds:

> He rode the subway up to Inwood, out to Sheepshead Bay. There were serious men down there, rocking in the copper light. He saw chinamen, beggars, men who talked to God, men who lived on the trains, day and night, bruised with matted hair, asleep in patient bundles on the wicker seats. . . . The noise was pitched to a fury he located in the mind, a satisfying wave of rage and pain.

Why else do serious lonely people do such fearsome things? And what is serious loneliness?

Even on November 22, some were suspicious. They saw so many other possible reasons for killing John Kennedy.

But common sense wanted to trust what seemed obvious. That Oswald had done it; that he was solitary and unstable; that it had been a frustrated story he sought to tell. And it was a horror story. We knew much less about JFK then, but so many loved him because he had the humor, the charm, and the improv flair of a movie star. And he was young, too, at a time when youth was beating down the cultural doors.

Oswald was only twenty-four when he died, and in that short

space he had started off in so many directions that he was difficult to track or to bring into a plausible story. He had been a Marine; he had slipped away to Russia—he seemed to be pro-communist; he tried to marry one Russian woman and then jumped to another; the couple came back to America—apparently without any official examination—and this was during the Cold War. He went into the South and the Southeast; he was pro-Cuba, or he was not; he tried to kill a general—but he missed at short range with the rifle he was said to have used from the Book Depository. He was such a mess that people seemed to avoid him. But for a few minutes he had acted like a marksman in a movie. Was that lucky chance? Or unlucky? Surely in the wide-open spaces of America chance blows like the wind.

Allow that Americans have felt daunted on their frontier, by the emptiness, the extent, its lurking perils, and the metaphor of insignificance. Do people sometimes fire at the distance, to kill it or make it manageable? If that seems fanciful to you, consider how we need to fathom why kids fire guns in America. It can happen anywhere and nowhere:

> But then, in the earliest hours of that morning in November [1959], a Sunday morning, certain foreign sounds impinged on the normal nightly Holcomb noises—on the keening hysteria of coyotes, the dry scrape of scuttling tumbleweed, the racing, receding wail of locomotive whistles. At the time not a soul in sleeping Holcomb heard them—four shotgun blasts that, all told, ended six human lives. But afterward the townspeople, theretofore sufficiently unfearful of each other to seldom trouble to lock their doors, found fantasy re-creating them

over and again—those somber explosions that stimulated fires of mistrust in the glare of which many old neighbors viewed each other strangely, and as strangers.

That's from the opening section of Truman Capote's *In Cold Blood* (1965), an account of the murder of the Clutter family in Holcomb, Kansas, a marker in the realization that random murders, harsh but dull, were material for literature and cinema. There was a movie, in 1967, concentrating on the killers (played by Robert Blake and Scott Wilson). Then, decades later came two more films that recognized how Capote was an oblique accomplice in the crime or that strange looking that followed. In the first, *Capote*, Philip Seymour Hoffman upstaged the crime through his virtuoso impersonation. The second film, the lesser known *Infamous*, seems to me superior (with Daniel Craig and Lee Pace as the killers) because it is aware of the secret killer in Capote (so well played by Toby Jones), who had his great coup with the book, just like Peter Lorre on *M*, and then never recovered.

Oswald matched the killers in Holcomb, Kansas, emphatic yet blank. For much of two days in November 1963, he was held by the authorities—and interrogated. Yet no records survived of that, just hearsay from the cops, as if people were too excited to be professional? Then around 11:30 on the morning of the 24th, in the basement of the Dallas police station, a man stepped forward out of the crowd and shot Oswald dead as two cops were escorting him. So many of those who had clung to the lone gunman theory fell back in dismay. What could this be but conspiracy and design? Or was it another lone gunman? Had the hothead in Ruby—which is not madness—been inspired or propelled by what Oswald had done? Do killers copy earlier killers? Is the United States a train of such dangerous loners? It depended on what kind of story you felt, and whether American murder was a wind or a methodology.

Oswald and Ruby are emblems in our history. We can summon a close-up picture of them as easily as a television newscast could find the head shots to accompany an anniversary item. More to the point, both men have a crucial piece of film or coverage that is always used. Jack Ruby shot Oswald live on TV—it was NBC that covered it—and those desperate seconds linger, along with the theatrical surprise of what had just happened. The TV audience was horrified (of course), but we felt delivered or lucky to have caught it. I know, that word "lucky" is shocking. You want to resist it. But recognize how we have been raised to anticipate disaster in watching news.

The movie link to Oswald has other levels. When Kennedy was shot, a bystander in Dealey Plaza, Abraham Zapruder, was filming the event on his 8mm Bell & Howell movie camera. He was defined by his camera, where he was standing, the passage of the motorcade, and his neutrality—he was his camera, no more.

That footage (486 frames, or 26.6 seconds) became essential evidence in the furious and unending inquiry on the president's death, and the model of all the stories that would be told about it. Everyone saw it, and analyzed the frames in order, especially the puff of light and membrane where Kennedy's head exploded: *Life* magazine bought the film for $150,000. And we reckoned we had seen enough Westerns and war films to "know" how bodies recoiled.

The film was factual, it was an object; it was even the truth twenty-four times a second (as Jean-Luc Godard had pronounced in his fatuous authority). But that truth was less than decisive or even helpful. And in Zapruder's camera it was eighteen frames a second. No one was ever certain what the strip of film said. And later, when putative soundtracks of the key moments were added, the "truth" became even more elusive. The murders of Kennedy and Oswald were commanding events in history—they had happened. But they were also part of a mounting fictional tumult in which we faced the disappearance of certainty. You could say this was paranoia, but it amounted to creative expression, too. As a statistic, murder was in decline in the West—but as a foreboding it was everywhere.

Murder had become a possibility and an atmosphere and a terrible mood in which lost individuals might register their existence and how they felt overlooked. The idea of murder is a direct signal of our destroyed politics, and in that regard the murderer has become a waiting outsider.

FEMME FATALE

If there is a Lee Oswald type, a figure in our mythology, why are there no female Oswalds yet—or will there be? It's not as if women lack cause for anger or alienation from our society.

Take Alex Forrest in *Fatal Attraction* (1987), that spectacular show of feminist urges in a mainstream picture made to goose the guys. Alex is branded as "fatal," but she is the only person killed. Before I'd seen the film a friend in the business had told me: "It's every man's worst nightmare." He said this with delight and promise. For the story is built on a male dream of going wild and being forgiven. The Michael Douglas character is set up as an urbane gentleman outlaw. After all, he's in publishing.

Alex (Glenn Close) was a knockout in 1987—she had some of the best hair in cinema. (We can't quite say "knockout" now, but the word was alive and well as the film was made.) She is erotically alert—the sex scenes are not just exciting and beyond decorum. They cherish illicit seduction as a fuel in our life. Infidelity is keeping the faith, just as real kisses are stolen. Equal credit for that goes to Douglas (Dan) and his unerring understanding of the American prick at liberty when Dan's nice family go off to the country for a weekend.

That's how he meets Alex. He can see she wants him, and he yields to that opportunity. An interesting question about the picture is, does Alex love Dan, or does she just need a sexy weekend (same as Dan). Why not? It should be a part of feminism that men have learned women have a right to adventure. But then Alex hates to end their fling. Is she in love—or is she possessive? Or, does she not buy into the standard male arrangement of getting to have sex with a woman by indicating that he's in love with her?

Fatal Attraction—written by James Dearden, directed by Adrian Lyne—is from a male point of view. The film doesn't allow Alex any rights, and it's afraid of admitting that profound love can make someone irrational. But her hair signals a wildness that might go out of control. The original ending, written and shot, had Alex killing herself in Dan's house, because she felt lost and abandoned. But the guys in charge of the film were uneasy with that, so they proposed a change. Glenn Close was unhappy that Alex now turned nightmarish, letting Dan and his wife (Anne Archer) come together to kill her. The only killing Alex got to do was a rabbit.

Women do not have equality in the general matter of murder. We may assume that they don't want to do it, that they are less innately violent. (But they lack so many rights as yet.) When it comes to our mass shootings, only two percent of those killers are female. With murder in general, women are killers just ten percent of the time. Not that they don't have motivation, whether spurned like Alex Forrest, or beaten at home like Farrah Fawcett's character in *The Burning Bed* (1984). After thirteen years of abuse, that woman makes a pyre of her husband—and is acquitted on murder charges because of temporary insanity. Not that thirteen years is temporary; not that what she did was unreasonable.

Lizzie Borden may have chopped up her father and her stepmother in Massachusetts in 1892 (she got off). There is a TV movie of the story, from 1975, with Elizabeth Montgomery, and now there is *Lizzie* with Chloë Sevigny as the killer and Kristen Stewart as her lover. But in that era, women in their traps were more inclined to put poison in the coffee than find an axe, or a gun. Is that more ladylike, or just domesticity? *Madeleine* (1950) is less known than it should be, though directed by David Lean. It was based on actual events in Glasgow in the 1850s, when a respectable young woman was charged with poisoning her lover. The woman was played by Lean's wife, Ann Todd, a rather cold blonde with a brittle intensity. The film's use of her and the furtive household where the events occurred is impeccable. And it stays true to the actual verdict, "not proven," a measure still available in the Scottish courts that says, well, really, we're not sure—which dramatically is too sophisticated for most motion pictures, where the urge to finish tidily is important.

"Not proven" could apply to Bette Davis's Leslie Crosbie in

The Letter (1940). As that film opens, she fires six bullets into a man on the verandah of her Malayan plantation house. She will tell the authorities that he came to her house at night while her husband was away and was about to rape her. The truth comes out slowly: Leslie was infatuated with the man who was ending their affair, so she shot him in the sexual temper that went with Bette's eyes and seemed ready to jump out of her melodramatic face. Six bullets: there's a passion in firing. *The Letter* still works, but if you were going to remake it now, it might be best to have Leslie disenchanted as much as dumped. Let her shoot the man because of some deep-seated regret over her life and being alone in Malaya.

That is not too far from Amy (Rosamund Pike) in *Gone Girl* (2014), a onetime perfect girl who has grown weary of life, of romance, without much hope of anything. She was a prizewinning kid, the subject of "Amazing Amy" children's books, published by her parents. But life has let her down and left a vague viciousness. It's another David Fincher film, from a novel by Gillian Flynn, and most upsetting in the scene where Amy slaughters an ex-beau (Neil Patrick Harris) in bed. Amy has a plot in mind, as preposterous as an Agatha Christie. But in Fincher's gaze the lavish murder, with Amy wreathed in blood, seems as unnervingly spiritual as Janet Leigh in *Psycho*'s bathroom.

Amy has set up her complicated plot not really for money, or out of malice toward her husband. She thinks she will commit suicide when it is all over. The real murder victim is any hope for the thing called marriage. Flynn did her own screenplay and was clear that she wanted a woman to be bad, violent, and in control.

Rosamund Pike was nominated for that work, and murderous women have fared well at the Oscars. Gene Tierney dropped her customary bland beauty to be homicidal in *Leave Her to Heaven* (1945), a film with disturbing Technicolor insights into how a romantic ideal in mid-America could unhinge or liberate a jealous woman. Anjelica Huston was so good as the mother who killed her son in *The Grifters* (1991) that the question hangs in the air—was it an accident or did she know what she was doing? Barbara Stanwyck is alluring in *Double Indemnity* (1944) as Phyllis, an unscrupulous conniver, a movie flirt, and someone who has used Fred MacMurray, but she's never exactly mad despite a tendency in the film and the James M. Cain novel to have her lose her mind in fury or plain evil. Phyllis is just trying to get ahead. She needs to be out of her drab marriage; she wants money and adequate sex; and she wants to feel in charge—what's mad about that, fellows?

All of those performances were nominated. But two murderesses have won the full Oscar. In *I Want to Live* (1958), Susan Hayward was Barbara Graham, who had been executed in the gas chamber in 1955 for her part in a gang robbery-killing. The movie was raw and strident in its case against capital punishment and wrongful conviction, but Hayward in her own research reached the conclusion that "Bloody Babs" had really been guilty.

That film has dated badly, because of its underlined message and because dreadful lives were then more sanitized on screen. Patty Jenkins's *Monster* (2003) is still alive or active in our minds. Few doubted that Charlize Theron, one of the most beautiful women on screen, would get an Oscar for transforming herself into Aileen Wuornos.

Wuornos had been executed in 2002 in Florida for six murders. She was a low-class, vagrant prostitute, often beaten up or raped, a lesbian probably, a physical wreck, swollen, unclean and derelict. Theron took on the role with a vengeance. She put on thirty pounds, wore bad false teeth and made herself ecstatically unattractive. (What few knew then was that Theron had her own history of being abused.) The physicality she achieved was so startling it tended to stop one thinking about a woman driven to tormented extremes in part because she does not look like Charlize Theron.

Still, it can be hard for a mainstream picture to go all the way. *Bonnie and Clyde* (1967) remains famous for its celebration of outlawry, or going wild. It was a lyrically violent picture. Faye Dunaway is fashion-plate unruly as Bonnie because even on the dusty backroads of Oklahoma and Texas she seems to have access to a beauty parlor. She got nominated for a fresh level of glamorous recklessness in movie women. She is also the best brain in her outfit and its most sexually urgent member. She wants sex much more than Clyde. Bonnie understands where they are going, and she writes the ballad about them for the newspaper.

That at last gives Clyde a hard-on because "You told my story." Not her story. Bonnie is sane and professional, and if you watch the action closely, you detect a kind of tenderness towards her, in part commercial and cosmetic, but romantic too, so that Bonnie never quite has to kill anyone.

Perhaps you find it disconcerting if I encourage a fairer shake for women in the matter of murder. There has been a fixed convention that women are the threatened sexual targets of rapists and serial killers—in fact, that fate occurs more often on screen than in life, and it testifies to a male fear of women that is at the heart of so many American maladies. You wonder sometimes how girlfriends are sitting obediently in the movie dark with their guys watching franchises roll by in which women are stripped of clothing, courage, dignity, and life in scenes of a violence that ought to be outrageous. There are women who will not watch rape scenes on the principle that enactments of rape induce imitation. In the age of *The Big Sleep*, smoking on screen worked in a similar way. That could be the start of a kind of censorship (or self-control) that undermines cinema itself. But I'm no longer sure that that would be such a loss.

Long ago now, in the aftermath of *Psycho*, Roman Polanski made a film in London, *Repulsion* (1966), that touched on the way a beautiful but inhibited woman, Carol (Catherine Deneuve), might run amok because of the sexual pressure of male expectations. In turn, Carol kills a couple of men in her house in Battersea, all in black and white, in what is often classified as a horror

film. But history overlooks the title of the movie: Carol is re-
pulsed by heartless male attention to a point where she reacts.
That's not so far from Aileen Wuornos.

We feel we know Polanski's history with sex and violence—
and after forty years, in 2018, he was expelled from the ridiculous Academy for being a bad boy. (They had given him an
Oscar for directing *The Pianist* when he was just as bad.) He was
never a sweetheart—but the list of sweetheart film directors is
on a blank page at the end of this book. He is a remarkable filmmaker, always on the run since childhood, and while he is lost to
America (where he made *Chinatown*), he does demonstrate how
murder can be handled more shrewdly in Europe.

François Truffaut adored women, and he often announced
that that desire was the essence of cinema. So male voyeurism
and promiscuity might be a philosophy. But he never shrank
from a darker side in women that came close to fatalism and
destructive instincts. *Jules and Jim* (1962) was sometimes hailed
as a blithe view of a ménage à trois, but its heroine, Catherine
(Jeanne Moreau), is unhappy for long stretches, and seldom relaxed. She sees the shallowness in male affection, and the dead
end in romance. Catherine is tougher minded than her guys.
She is growing older and she has become gloomy and solitary—
that dead end was always in Moreau's screen persona. At the close
of the film, with casual aplomb, she kills herself and Jim. He is
not a willing partner in this, but he is murdered, fondly, as if to
say life has let Catherine down.

In *The Soft Skin* (1964), a wronged wife marches into a restaurant where her faithless husband is eating lunch and shoots him dead with a shotgun. He was too feeble and dishonest for her, but her violence is not just anecdotal. It is the most striking thing in a rather minor film. Then in *The Bride Wore Black* (1968), Julie (Moreau again) sets out to murder (or execute) the five men who were responsible for her husband's death. It is not a good film, and Moreau does little more than be implacable, but it was Truffaut working in the manner of Hitchcock, the director he had done so much to celebrate.

Far more impressive is *Mississippi Mermaid* (1969), where Catherine Deneuve plays a wandering criminal and opportunist. She has helped murder the mail-order bride who was on her way to marry Louis (Jean-Paul Belmondo) on the island of Réunion in the Indian Ocean. He is a rich man and Julie marries him. He knows she is wrong, but decides not to notice; so he is an accomplice in her scheme. Louis believes he is in bliss. Then she steals his money and runs back to Europe. He follows her and finds her. She confesses to her crimes and her wretched life and they seem in love again. They even join in the killing of a private detective Louis had hired to find her. But then she tries to kill Louis. She wants to be free, yet she is helpless when she is with him. Her own mind is not proven. It is a portrait of a woman who can be quite matter-of-fact, for whom killing is secondary to both love and despair. Men think a femme fatale is out to get them, but the dark women know they are simply on their own way to death.

Perhaps the strength of these films depends on the fortitude and the status of their actresses. Moreau and Deneuve were stars in France, and so many of their films are love stories of one kind or another. They were believed by their audience, and that made them brave enough to take on roles that were far from simply likable.

No one fits that definition better than Isabelle Huppert. In 1978, when she was twenty-five and had made a dozen films already, she was cast by director Claude Chabrol as the eighteen-year-old *Violette Nozière*. As a teenage prostitute, Violette murders her father (by poison) and then alleges in the trial that he had molested her. We never know how credible her story is—or whether it would justify murder. In life, the real Nozière was convicted and sentenced to the guillotine. But she was spared that and after commutation she eventually left prison, married, and became the mother of five. Today, one wishes that later life could have been part of Chabrol's film, with Huppert as alive and enigmatic as she is in *La Cérémonie*, *The Piano Teacher*, or *Elle*. She and Sandrine Bonnaire played joint murderesses in *La Cérémonie* (and they shared the Volpi Cup for acting at the Venice Film Festival), but elsewhere Huppert has been a mistress at killing with a glance, or a shrug.

There is an English film I'd like to mention, which has no faith in being "nice." *Longford* (2008) was a television movie, directed by Tom Hooper and written by Peter Morgan. Its title character is Lord Longford (Jim Broadbent), who devoted much of his time to prison reform and the rehabilitation of criminals. One of his subjects was Myra Hindley (Samantha Morton), who with Ian Brady (Andy Serkis) carried out the infamous Moors murders. In the mid-1960s, in the rural area outside Manchester, Brady and Hindley captured, tortured, and murdered five children. They buried the corpses on the moors. These murders horrified and enthralled Britain, and indicated the disorder beneath polite facades.

Both killers would die in captivity, Brady as recently as 2017. But Longford visited Hindley in Holloway prison, and in their developing relationship he sought her parole. She had made herself popular in the prison. She was amiable with Longford. Was she rehabilitated, or was she using him? Did she deserve parole? Would Britain have allowed it? It's another case of not proven. In the process Morton gives a rendering of the murderess as banal yet mysterious, but not as frightening as Serkis's Brady, who delivers evil in fifteen minutes—and Serkis was on his way to being Caesar, our great rogue ape. Lord Longford was widely mocked in Britain for his naïveté and sentimentality, while Hindley (who did not look like Samantha Morton) became a brand image of female wickedness.

It can be hard for professional actresses, raised to be lovely and obliging, to play such dark figures. One actress has been curiously involved in the refrain of murder. As an adolescent, Jodie Foster played the prostitute who prompts Travis Bickle's violence in *Taxi Driver*. (She was given counseling at the time to be sure she could handle the small massacre her character had witnessed.) It was clear that she was an exceptional actress with unusual intellectual capacity. While she was at Yale she learned that she was an obsessive focus for John Hinckley as he tried to kill President Reagan. Hinckley said he had wanted to impress Foster. She said she was a "hapless bystander" in that interaction, but she was smart enough to know that movie rapture can encourage disturbed fantasies.

Hinckley was released from detention in 2016 and ordered to live with his mother (she was ninety). He cannot go near Foster; he is limited to a range of fifty miles from where he lives in Virginia; he cannot possess weapons, alcohol, or pornography, and his Internet usage is restricted. In 2018, it was agreed that he could live on his own. These measures may be secure and enlightened. But they seem like the backstory to a horror film.

As an adult, Foster became a prominent American heroine: she won her first Oscar as the raped woman in *The Accused* (1988), and then a second as Clarice, the FBI agent who is under threat in *The Silence of the Lambs* (1991), and who arouses a sickly affection in Hannibal Lecter. Despite her success, Foster did not easily find her way in conventional romantic films. She was "attractive"; she sometimes posed for glamour photographs; but something in her being seemed withheld, or clenched. It was not quite in her acting nature to be beguiling, but she was in her element as a threatened woman (and mother) in *Panic Room* (2002). In time, she would reveal her own lesbian life.

That is some background to Neil Jordan's picture *The Brave One* (2007), where Foster plays a woman who is walking with her lover one night in Central Park when three hoodlums attack them. The lover is murdered and Erica is so traumatized that she buys a gun for herself—as if mindful of those politicians who say the only way to treat gun violence is to get yourself a weapon. Erica kills several people, with some justification. But the vigilante mood is beginning to consume or unbalance her. She starts talking to a police detective (Terrence Howard) in scenes that go deeper into female victimhood and its wounded response than all the films that cheerfully cater to rape and revenge.

Erica's bravery is ambiguous; she is a heroine and a criminal; it is as if the law itself has let her down. The femme fatale was once a stock character in genre mythology. Her nastiness gave spice to sex itself. But it has long been time to recognize the damage that the myth has done to real women well aware of their inevitable demise.

THE WOODMAN'S BRIGHT AXE

I have suggested how watching a movie puts us the viewers in a perilously superior position to the action. Call it the overlook, or a cold-blooded seat of judgment, so that the warm, "very human" antics of the characters are placed or isolated in the cool glow of the streaming, like items in a game we are free to play with. Thus murders can become mere actions or gestures, moves instead of moral events of unalterable consequence and damage.

If that condition has affected us over a century, and spread a kind of indifference or detachment, imagine what the same climate can do to filmmakers, especially those whose track record or commercial status involves delivering satisfying murders—people like Hitchcock, of course, or David Fincher, or even Woody Allen.

For decades that last name would have seemed surprising in this context. Wasn't Allen famous, and adored, as a comic, a funny man, as amiable as anyone hoping to make us laugh? Moreover, it became apparent that our Woody—he really was ours for so long—was the most reliable movie director around. Forget director's block or budgetary restrictions, give up on possible neurosis in being a genius or an auteur, Woody Allen's fixation was to produce at least one film a year, for ever and forever. He knew, and we accepted, that the quality would fluctuate. He was doing pictures as steadily as Bonnard painted his wife in the bath. So wait a few months and here was another Woodman picture.

Some of them were funny and intriguing. There were masterworks, like *Radio Days* and *The Purple Rose of Cairo*. But the consistency was in the fertile rearrangement of story situations with vivid characters who were seldom embraced by the films or their maker. Those people went past in a lively blur, just as Bonnard seldom bothered to show us his wife's face. You wondered if Allen wasn't an auteur surveying all his people without needing to like them or be hurt with them, as if he even disdained them a little because they were his playthings, his chess pieces.

We like to think our comics are good-hearted and endearing, so Allen's chill gaze wasn't much remarked on. But two films emerged from the busy body of his work—*Crimes and Misdemeanors* (1989) and *Match Point* (2005)—as if to say, in truth, he had scant interest in being merely comic.

They are disconcerting pictures with central characters driven to commit murders: in *Crimes and Misdemeanors*, Judah (Martin Landau) removes his mistress Dolores (Anjelica Huston) because her neediness threatens the fake order of his respectable life. In

Match Point a similar thing happens when Chris (Jonathan Rhys Meyers) murders his lover Nola (Scarlett Johansson), and one unlucky observer, to preserve his shaky status quo.

It is not that guilt does not affect these killers. But then that negativity is overcome or absorbed. On police terms, the two crimes are settled and explained. The murderers remain innocent parties. Life goes on, and there is no sign that they are slowed or even limping from the damage they have done to themselves, the world, or the ambience of our spectatorship.

Moral damage can be accommodated. But we may wonder how far that adjustment has been assisted by the benefits of our overlook. Don't we often observe faraway disaster and tragedy these days in the same uninvolved way? Like insurance investigators? But there is a raw anguish in Huston's Dolores, and Allen never did a love scene as hot or urgent—as moving—as the one with Scarlett Johansson and Rhys Meyers in a field of corn. It was so startling when that film opened to see Woody's passion. One realized how secretive he had been for so long.

And then those women were blown away like brief flowers. They were murdered, or removed. Ardent romantics sometimes find old beloveds in their way, and they begin to storyboard escape. This goes back in movie history to *A Place in the Sun* (1951), where Montgomery Clift's character goes to the electric chair not because he did kill his pregnant girlfriend (Shelley Winters), who impeded his "true" love with Elizabeth Taylor, but because he wanted Winters out of the way.

Murder may be less common now in dead love affairs and

stranded marriages. And not just because of divorce's oil. We have found other ways of being together yet in a state of removal. We are not always there in our lives; we are watching them. The Woodman is never quite sure whether this is a malady or a comedy.

SLAUGHTER

It is tempting in studying history or living one's life to put some faith in one thing causing another. But often too much is going on for us to be that organized or clear. One murder may seem to prompt another: when Sollozzo tried to kill Vito Corleone, he knew what to expect in response. But suppose Vito had been hit by a car moments before the assassin could get to him. Think of the set piece story going off in untidy but lifelike ways. Remember how Gavrilo Princip shot the archduke and his wife late in the afternoon in 1914, when he thought the big plan had failed, when the driver of the royal car got lost and took an unlucky turn. Or was it lucky?

Murder wants to be a drastic, dramatic assertion of man's power—but it does not heal the humbling knowledge that everyone will die in some kind of confusion.

Tidiness can become a prison, and a merciless tit for tat. A useful source of understanding is staying uncertain over what has happened. But we are drawn to art and story because of their urge to make reliable connections. So we can be caught in a sequence of murders, the kind of progression that operated in Agatha Christie's *Ten Little Niggers* (published with that title in 1939), which had to be reassessed as *And Then There Were None*, but which remains a classic construct of elimination by murder.

I am writing this in 2018, in the immediate aftermath of the killings at the Santa Fe High School in Texas, where eight students and two teachers were shot dead—ten young people. The interpretations of that event were so many that they undermined response. This is by now a script we feel we know by heart—or is it buried in us? Some state governor says that we should all have a roundtable gathering and put forward our views—as if that had not been done before; as if the elements of tragedy were not naked. Another proposes that schools should have fewer entrances and exits—perhaps none at all? If you eliminated schools, wouldn't that solve school shootings? There are those who urge that teachers be armed. Why not students, too? Some say every last firearm in the United States should be broken and forgotten. Sooner or later, it is determined that some kid killers have been abused, badly raised, miseducated, misunderstood. Maybe they are mad? But does "mad" mean angry, or simply outside the common, shared compound of what is factual, reasonable, or sensible in this America? Why is it that the land of the free and the home of the brave is so crowded with this aloneness? Is it the fact of the guns, and the fear they represent? Is it the cameras shooting? Or is it the remorseless pressure to be brave? Can't we admit we are afraid?

Charles Whitman had the appearance of a fine guy. He was blond, vigorous, and what is called good-looking. He had been the youngest Eagle Scout in America, and he had a high I.Q. He had been a Marine. He was a thoughtful young man. In advance of what happened, he purchased a knife, a pair of binoculars, and a can of Spam, for he foresaw that he would need provisions just like Robinson Crusoe or Seaman Albert Brown on his island. He also asked that after his death his brain could be examined because he suspected something was wrong. He typed up a note:

> I do not quite understand what it is that prompts me to type this letter. Perhaps it is to leave some vague reason for the actions I have recently performed. I do not really understand myself these days. I am supposed to be an average reasonable and intelligent young man. However, lately (I can't recall when it started) I have been a victim of many unusual and irrational thoughts. These thoughts constantly recur, and it requires a tremendous mental effort to concentrate on useful and progressive tasks.

In the summer of 1966, Whitman was twenty-five and living in Austin, Texas. The "actions I have recently performed" were the murder of his mother and his wife. There is no reason to doubt his claim that he loved both of them. Love is in the eye of a beholder, even if it's taking aim. Whitman's dad had been a hard man: he taught his son to shoot, but he sometimes beat the boy and his own wife. She had lately faced up to her need to divorce him and that ordeal had given Charlie bad headaches.

In the early hours of August 1, he seems to have smothered his mom as she slept and stabbed her in the heart. He then moved on and killed his wife in a similar way. He made telephone calls to say that neither woman would be at work that day. He put together a backpack of his binoculars, the Spam, and coffee, along with toilet paper and deodorant. He also had several weapons just purchased, including a Remington hunting rifle with sights. Then he climbed the landmark tower at the center of the Austin campus of the University of Texas and reached the observation deck, about 300 feet high. Just before noon, from that overlook, he started to fire on people below. He killed eighteen (that number included an unborn child) and wounded thirty-one. At 1:25 P.M. two policemen reached the observation deck and shot and killed Whitman.

An autopsy was performed. The first report saw no obvious causes for Whitman's behavior. A second inquiry found a small tumor in his brain, but there was uncertainty over how conclusive that was. Whitman had told doctors in the months before August 1 that he had had inexplicable urges to violence, and they may have come from the tumor. When John Berryman wrote his "Dream Song" about Whitman (no. 135), he spoke of the tumor "thudding in his brain." But in 1966 no medical estimate could be sure of that. Perhaps he was ill, or just unhappy. Or was the event the result of his uncertainty in life being allied to the availability of guns, to the tower, to our deep-seated dismay? Would it have made a difference if the university had employed armed guards on the observation deck? Or would better teaching at the university have helped? Did the mother and the wife need to go without sleep and stay armed at all times? We do not know. We have to be confounded by the event itself. To be alive you need to go to sleep sometimes.

But intelligence yearns to find connecting answers. Life seems reasonable only if those links work. Just two years after the outrage in Austin an ingenious if opportunistic film appeared, called *Targets* (1968). It came from Peter Bogdanovich and his wife Polly Platt. He was a critic-journalist on movies, longing to be a director. He wangled his chance from the producer Roger Corman, who was owed two days' work from Boris Karloff and had spare footage from a Karloff film, *The Terror.* Add in a little more than $100,000. Could Bogdanovich make that work?

He and Platt came up with a proposal that was downright glib, but so clever. There would be two stories: Byron Orlok (Karloff, naturally) would be an aging horror actor, disenchanted with his own genre; for the other story, there was a numb Whitmanesque guy (played by Tim O'Kelly) who killed his wife and mother and then found a high vantage (on top of a fuel container) and started shooting people. But the two stories had to collide, so the young man on the run hides out at a movie theatre where Orlok is making an appearance. The kid shoots through the screen at people, but Orlok trounces him. Aren't movie stars wonderful? All done in ninety minutes, and so cunning that Robert Evans took it up to be released by Paramount.

It's the sort of B picture a smart film critic might make given the chance, and I don't mean to knock it, because the idea of horror masking a real situation that affects people is valid, and the idea of shooting the audience through the screen is promising black comedy. Bogdanovich was launched on a career. Tim O'Kelly was barely heard of again. Karloff died less than a year later. Rather than address the problem, *Targets* helped foster the genre of a lone killer.

There is another film to mention, though it has been very little seen—it played in thirteen theatres. *Tower* (2016) was made by Keith Maitland, who had been a student at Austin. Based on a magazine article, "96 Minutes," by Pamela Colloff, on the larger context provoked by Charles Whitman, it is a documentary about the range of people who were caught up in the shootings, as victims, cops, or bystanders. It has documentary footage, as well as rotoscope animation of the action. The marvel of *Tower* is that this way of seeing alters our perspective on the outrage and reduces or raises it to a level of ordinary life. Most who saw the film admired it, or loved it, but it did very little business—as if to warn moviemakers, just keep our mass killings straight and concentrate on the killer, please.

In Santa Fe, Texas, the mourning goes on, and I suppose there will be earnest roundtable talks. For a moment, everyone in America knows the face of the young murderer from his Facebook picture. The name is harder than the face: Dimitrios Pagourtzis—we may not learn to spell that before another killer comes along. He killed kids he knew, and it's possible that he was bullied at school, mocked or ostracized by some of those students. School can be like that. But school has a new intimidation now in which some students wonder when their school will have its assassin, and how to run in a zig-zag pattern to escape the bullets.

By the time this book appears, Santa Fe will have reverted to being the place in New Mexico, and you will have forgotten the face of the youth who caused the rampage in Texas. When are governors going to stop promising discussions to ensure that such things "never happen again"? We are in a winter of fatigue and nihilism that believes such crises will occur over and over to a point where "crisis" is no longer the apt word. If you feel offended by that, or disconcerted by its bleakness, if you insist your memory is loyal, then try to recall the name of the young man who was the murderer at Sandy Hook.

There are some commentators who believe these murderers should not be named, or have their pictures put up on the television screens—as if that brief attention is what motivates them. As if fame were un-American. It may be that some people want to break out of the dark and lonely underworld of being unknown in a country that sings all the time about fame. Then recall how many of them kill themselves in the last gesture of the outrage and consider the despair in that premeditation. Such killings are suicidal, or as if impelled by a feeling that the world is dead already, or a game in which one may be known by a kill count.

Sandy Hook was the Sandy Hook Elementary School in Newtown, Connecticut. On the morning of December 14, 2012, the twenty-year-old Adam Lanza (who had attended it as a child) broke into the school and began to use his mother's Bushmaster XM15-E2S rifle, a semiautomatic weapon that could fire forty-five rounds per minute. He had taken the gun from his mother, who was a gun enthusiast and had a dozen or so in the house she shared with Adam. He had also killed his mother with the gun.

He murdered twenty children and six adults at the school, then killed himself. Should we remember him—or defy his terrible attempt to break as our news?

We know quite a lot about Adam Lanza, and it's disturbing as a version of knowledge. At twenty, he was a gaunt beanpole, six feet and 112 pounds. In the picture that was put out, he has staring eyes—or was that a look he was doing for fun in the way kids goose the camera in selfies? He was suffering from anorexia; he had been diagnosed with Asperger's; and there were reports of mounting anxiety and compulsive disorders. He changed his socks twenty times a day; he was always washing his hands; he would not let his mother or daylight in his room; he had no friends. He was said to be obsessed with previous mass killings at schools, notably the 1999 shooting at Columbine High School in Colorado, where fifteen people died, including the two shooters. For hours on end Lanza played World of Warcraft on his computer. He lived in the same house as his mother but communicated with her through e-mail.

Tell me when you're too distressed—or is this list of symptomatic conditions too like a character study or the description of someone in a movie? Adam had had no treatment and very little systematic education for years before Sandy Hook. His parents lived apart and he had uncertain contact with his father and his brother. But did he have better contact with his mother—or with anyone? So is there a law against being solitary or on some Resolution?

Is it proper to call him "Adam"? Should I stick with Lanza, or simply write him off as "the killer" or "the murderer," or some John Doe? Can you name one of the children killed at Sandy Hook? Is that failure trivial or irrelevant, or does it tell us something about ourselves and our shadow—the interest in murderers? Do you know who Albert DeSalvo was or why you might be reproached for not knowing?

Does the hashtag "Boston strangler" clear the air? There were a number of murders in Boston in the early 1960s. The victims were women; the modus operandi involved strangling or knives. The press in that city announced the existence of a "mad Boston strangler," and Albert DeSalvo confessed. There was evidence against him in at least some of the cases. A few women said they recognized him—*he* was the guy. But DeSalvo was charged with other offenses—rapes, not murder. Still, the possibility that he was the Strangler clouded his trial: it was like a movie he had been in, another life. He was sentenced to life imprisonment in 1967. But he escaped from Bridgewater State Hospital, where he was being held. He said this was to expose the bad conditions in that place. Then he gave himself up and was sent to Walpole State Prison. Six years later, he was murdered in that prison. No one has ever been charged for that crime.

There were doubts from the start. Some saw DeSalvo as a

disturbed personality who was attaching himself to the "mad strangler" reputation. Some experts who examined him believed he was desperate for attention, and for the lurid identity of being the strangler. Our fascination with killers was all very well, but another archetype was emerging—that of some ghost in the dark who might find celebrity, life, and even purpose by being known as an M.

Just a year after DeSalvo's conviction on a series of rape charges, a film appeared, *The Boston Strangler*, written by Edward Anhalt from a well-researched book by Gerold Frank, directed by Richard Fleischer, with Tony Curtis as DeSalvo. The concept of the film was that DeSalvo had a split personality, the strangler and the regular guy. In the course of the action, a psychiatrist gets him to recognize the split and to be horrified by it. It is a film gimmicked up by split screens as well as split personality.

But we appreciate that scheme: it's Jekyll and Hyde, good and bad; it's that bipolar tendency in people who have not been officially diagnosed. It's a cover-all reading for anything we may want to do. It's as tempting as being in the movie theatre and pretending you are on the screen.

Curtis got the part by altering his appearance enough to slip past the legend of that pretty "Tony Curtis." Yet the project needed a star—"Tony Curtis" overcame its ugly potential. Nearly every actor knows he can play a psychopath or a schizoid personality. That's how they learn their lines while talking to a real lover. Curtis said that his necessary anger or unlikability in the role was supplied by his bitter ongoing rift with his wife, Christine Kaufmann. He won the Golden Globe for his performance.

It's a dumb movie. The possibility that DeSalvo was all along pretending to be the Strangler—and that the Strangler legend may have comprised several different stranglers looking for a capital letter—was more intriguing than the old Jekyll and Hyde ping-pong. In the *New York Times*, Renata Adler said that the film "represents an incredible collapse of taste, judgment, decency, prose, insight, journalism and movie technique." All of which spoke to the culture's dire confusion over murder. The picture earned $17 million, four times what it cost.

It is as hard for an American movie to stand for cultural indecision as it is to leave a plot open. We need to know that Verbal Kint *is* Keyser Söze in *The Usual Suspects*. Like commercials, most pictures are pledged to calm, optimism, and single-mindedness. There are business pressures so set on confidence that audiences at large have moved away from murder mysteries or whodunits. David Fincher's *Zodiac* understands that a murderer's career is less important than the ways he is perceived by the society around him. So the film never quite pins the crimes on anyone, despite one riveting moment of apparent identification, but it concentrates on three imperfect lives—of a cop, a journalist, and a cartoonist—that are shaped by their preoccupation with the murders. And it is on the desolate Californian highways, at night, that murder can be as close as the car behind you. So much of *Zodiac*'s atmosphere has to do with aloneness.

Better still is *Taxi Driver* (1976), written by Paul Schrader, directed by Martin Scorsese, and with Robert De Niro as Travis Bickle. This is a savage yet deeply romantic evocation of New York City where the burnished colors and the steam escaping from the subway are married to Bernard Herrmann's beautiful yet vengeful music. It is a searing portrait of a lost soul, a would-be saint, a Vietnam wreck, a man uncertain how to go mad but drawn to it, and a dangerous, likely killer.

Schrader's script reads like a novel. It includes Travis's voice-over (inspired by the journal of Arthur Bremer, who had tried to murder George Wallace in 1972) and is as good as any inner movie voice:

> All my life needed was a sense of direction, a sense of someplace to go. I do not believe one should devote his life to morbid self-attention, but should become a person like other people.

In extremis, Travis thinks of saving a maybe-fourteen hooker (Jodie Foster). In that process he murders three people, and it is up to us to decide how justified or deranged he is. The killings are viewed with a kid's awe, but they were as terrible as killings had been on screen. They showed us just how far censoring restraints had given up on violence—though Scorsese was persuaded to desaturate the red of the blood to help the film get an R rating.

Again, Schrader knew where the film was going. In a footnote to the published script, and as a Calvinist always fixed on spiritual meaning, he added this:

The screenplay has been moving at a reasonably realistic level until the prolonged slaughter. The slaughter itself is a gory extension of violence, more surreal than real.

The slaughter is the moment Travis has been heading for all his life, and where the screenplay has been heading for over 85 pages. It is the release of all that cumulative pressure; it is a reality unto itself. It is the psychopath's Second Coming.

More disturbing still is the coda to the film in which this man deserving of confinement and the myth of treatment or rehab or even analysis is allowed to return to driving taxis, and to being the razor eyes watching us in the rearview mirror. There had never been a movie that so evoked our mixed feelings over murder and our unsteady hold on the thing we are supposed to revere, as members of its club—I am thinking about life and the dumb way it carries on.

President Trump is not alone in claiming that these lone, young killers are crazed, not human, and worthy of eradication et cetera. You would think our leading madman would show more genuine interest in mental disturbance. He might ask the rest of us to notice that these inhuman forces do keep getting access to guns, sometimes guns with video-game momentum. It is not so much social science as common sense to look at other "advanced" societies that have so much less taste for firearms and drastically fewer outrage shootings.

But there's a deeper malaise at work, and it can be assessed only in terms of culture and politics. Technically insane or not, some young people are in despair over their lives and the potential for life. They begin to shift towards the impersonality of electronic media that measure lives as digital hits. The aloneness is being institutionalized in systems that have abandoned personal contact. These are not "mental institutions," they are jobs, bureaucracy, social media, and the creep on artificial intelligence that could usher in artificial feelings. This might mean "relationships."

We are daunted at the emptiness of life and our futures. You can say that has to do with familial chaos, and an education that has left us helpless. So let the computers run our show. You can argue that we know the end of the world is coming, so let all else go hang. Isn't that the way a lot of rich people are behaving, living for tonight and tomorrow and speculating on next Thursday? We see so many enormous questions of human purpose failing through neglect and futility, and we put our lives at the same helpless level in a way that is hardly irrational. We know we will forget and be forgotten.

After the killings in the Pittsburgh synagogue in October 2018, David Brooks used his *New York Times* column to address "the lonely man" in America. By temperament, Brooks likes to think well of his fellow citizens, and to assume that he is not alone, but on October 30 he noted, "There's always one guy, who fell through the cracks of society, who lived a life of solitary disappointment and who one day decided to try to make a blood-drenched leap from insignificance to infamy."

That man may be a killer—or a writer.

Is that mood universal, or more American? Brooks linked it to what he called "surely one of the most shocking trends in America today": the suicide rate in the United States since 2000 has risen by thirty percent, with a special spike among teenage males.

A culture of death cannot be separated from our difficulty at believing in life. And it is idiocy to blame that on insanity. Brooks called it a sign of "the spreading derangement of the American mind." But maybe it is the imbalance in society and our politics. That speaks to a loss of faith in the American dream, the pursuit of happiness, and the promise that everything would be OK. That dismay is not crazy. It grows out of experience and calm observation.

THE ROOM I HAD TO LIVE IN

It is one of our tricks about being grown up that we reckon we can handle murder in a sophisticated way, taking it on the chin, recoiling and then coming back with our swift left hook. As if we were Sugar Ray Robinson? One potent deceit in movies is to make numb kids feel mature or capable. That's a root of gangsterese and murder stories.

In the late 1940s, on weekends, my father would take me to see athletics at the White City arena in London. We would get there on the Tube, and several times we saw the same beggar in the forecourt of the White City station. He was collapsed, a wraith in a blanket or an old coat, and he was so ravaged or so ill it was impossible to tell his age or how much longer he could live. There have always been these dead bodies not quite dead on our streets.

"That's Johnny Summers," Dad told me. "He was welter-weight champion of Britain once."

My father loved boxing. He had fought as an amateur and sparred with professional fighters. He gave me boxing gloves and told me to listen on the radio to the great Randolph Turpin–Sugar Ray fight in 1951, when Turpin won and was middleweight champion of the world for a couple of months. I did listen, and so did Dad, I think, though we were living on opposite sides of London.

What he told me about Summers was not quite true—but Dad was trying to teach me something about ambition by inventing a doomed character. The dead can guide our way. There had been a Johnny Summers (born in 1883), and he had been a champion. He had 164 fights, and won 96, huge numbers by modern standards. No wonder if he was punch drunk. He was welterweight champion for a time, but he died in 1946—a couple of years before I could have seen him at death's door. I don't know who our wraith was. I don't mind this error or Dad's pretense, or even feel it as such. So many boxers ended badly. Even the dazzling Sugar Ray Robinson was broke, with Alzheimer's, when he died. Dad's point was unfair but instructive.

His Summers story was meant to make me look beyond the glamour of reputation and being a champion. That's a severe test in cinema, where glamour can make murder shine and insecure people seem impregnable. We grow up searching for heroic figures, and cinema is a garden where those flowers grow. I mentioned the movie of *The Big Sleep* earlier, the one from 1946,

Hawks, with Bogart and Bacall. That noir ro-
ders, done with droll panache, as if to say a
nore cigarette. Tough guys can handle them.
strolls through the film as insouciant, attractive, and secure as America hoped to be in 1946.

There are movie people addicted to that attitude, and Bogart's
Philip Marlowe is a champ for us all. He can take a punch and
drop a wisecrack in a dame's lap; he'll kiss the sly beauty and then
shoot the villainous Canino when he has to. He's humble in his
way ($25 a day and expenses is all he asks), but he's enchanted
too, and still is, sixty years after Bogart perished from those cigarettes. Marlowe held the screen like American noir assurance,
but by 1957 Bogart was so diminished he was pulled upstairs and
down in his home in the dumbwaiter. We have loved him another sixty for his legend of laconic control; maybe that hope is
as treacherous as romantic cigarettes.

Except that that Bogart is not the entire Philip Marlowe.
There is also the book, by Raymond Chandler, published in
1939, and there are things there that didn't make it to the film,
like Chapter 24.

That's when Marlowe comes back to where he lives one night,
his home, a plain room in an apartment building. He doesn't live
like Humphrey Bogart in a big house with a dumbwaiter and
smart servants. He finds his bed is down—it's a Murphy bed that
folds into the wall—but the bed is down so Carmen Sternwood
can be in it, giggly and naked, "glistening as a pearl." In the movie,
Carmen is Martha Vickers. She's gorgeous and very amusing,

and as you watch the film you may reckon in your noir way you'd find twenty minutes for her, or as long as it took, without being driven mad.

Carmen simply provides herself for Marlowe in the book. She is depraved, a movie condition that can come with gorgeousness, and when he declines her offer she calls him "a filthy name." Perhaps he is a touch prim. Chandler doesn't fill us in: he had himself been to a school for gentlemen. But Marlowe has had enough of the Sternwoods, the whole murderous routine and the deadliness of its life. He tells himself with bitterness and even vengefulness:

> I didn't mind that. I didn't mind what she called me, what anybody called me. But this was the room I had to live in. It was all I had in the way of a home. In it was everything that was mine, that had any association for me, any past, anything that took the place of a family. Not much; a few books, pictures, radio, chessmen, old letters, stuff like that. Nothing. Such as they were they had all my memories.
>
> I couldn't stand her in that room any longer. What she called me only reminded me of that.

The film doesn't include this moment, because it's too grim or awkward for Hollywood. But the book makes it clear that Marlowe lives the life of a small-part actor desperate for a job. His aloneness is one of his precious things. On screen, Marlowe's solitude is superb and exemplary; in the book it feels vulnerable.

He gives Carmen three minutes to dress and get out of his home, the room that he lives in, and that's what she does. Alone, Marlowe "tore the bed to pieces savagely." You can find a willing and beautiful woman naked in your bed, asking for you, but somehow the ghost of Johnny Summers can be in there next to her, so you can't tell the two corpses apart.

This is a brief book about murder and the movies, or in the movies, or as an atmosphere that the movies have urged upon us. It could be an anthology of Great Movie Murders, the ideal gift book for the jolly aficionado in your family, some Uncle Charlie who gives you goose bumps reciting the honor roll of famous killings. To hear Uncle Charlie talk you could believe that murder is just a game of red rum. Here, have another, kid.

One of my favorites, he says, is Jack Vincennes in *L.A. Confidential* (1997). Vincennes is a cop in early 1950s Los Angeles who also advises television police shows. You can say that's a conflict of interests, but that's how Jack is, and no matter the conflict he is always interesting. Kevin Spacey plays Jack as the spirit of easygoing compromise, a man who has seen corpses cut to pieces at murder scenes (think of the desanguinated Black Dahlia from 1947) and then gives tips to *Dragnet*, or whatever, on the tasteful way of doing dead bodies. Jack is somewhere between Weegee and Fred Astaire. Everybody likes him, and that can mask his polished self-loathing. When director Curtis Hanson cast Spacey in the part, he told him to think of Dean Martin as his model.

To cut a long story short, Vincennes gets a breakthrough on the collection of cases the LAPD is dealing with in the early

1950s. In all innocence (a quality Spacey did with a mocking touch), he passes this news on to the chief, Captain Dudley Smith (James Cromwell). This happens in Dudley's kitchen, in the middle of the night. Jack is sitting in a chair and Dudley is making coffee for them. Whereupon—and this is done with ravishing suddenness—Smith takes out his gun and shoots Vincennes on the spot and in the chest. One shot. The blood starts to embroider Jack's white shirt. Just like that—breathtaking, in every sense. You see, the chief is the master of iniquity at the LAPD overlook. *He is the bad guy.*

Vincennes has seconds left to live. At which point, whatever you need to think about Kevin Spacey, the actor possesses those seconds in a way that bears watching forever—or for as long as you have. He shows astonishment, ingenuity, dread, and mischief, and he just manages to whisper a name ("Rollo Tomasi") that will haunt Dudley and ruin him. Those few seconds are a milestone in fatality, or life's last ebbing, yet enough to make you love Vincennes.

"Kevin Spacey. You gotta hand it to him!" says Uncle Charlie as he refills your glass.

Like Uncle Charlie, you will have your own favorites, and don't be aggrieved if they haven't been included in this book. There's no need for us to be in competition. As it is, it is my intention to give some broad sense of the myriad casualties. I am talking about those movies where untold numbers of human beings are destroyed or eliminated. That is a tradition that reaches from Fritz Lang's *Kriemhild's Revenge* (1924), still one of the best battle movies ever made, to whichever modern epic of slaughter has taken your fancy.

You may try to argue that battle scenes don't count as murder, but Uncle Charlie is sadder and wiser—he was gassed in the Great War in 1917 and was never the same again. That was a shocking war. He told me how he had been sleeping in a trench and one morning when it was still dark he woke up and a corpse was in his arms. It had eased out of the mud in the night.

We sometimes attribute such horrors to "senseless inhumanity," but Uncle Charlie and Jack Vincennes smile at that because they know it's all too human. And in that knowledge, we "know" the death toll in that Great War (for those of us in the church of counting) was somewhere between nine and eleven million military personnel and five or six million civilians. Those are sobering numbers that could drive you to drink, not least in letting us know that the plus or minus is about three million. Just contemplate what it would mean if first reports of a nuclear accident or a natural disaster came in with x million casualties— only to be amended a few days later with plus another 1.5 million. Overnight adjustment on an event that lasted 22 minutes, but a number that is a quarter of what we generally accept as the Holocaust total. Can you really feel the difference if, say, official revised estimates, after years of research, admitted that the Holocaust number ought to be 7.3 million?

The movies have found a technology that overrides the plus or minus, and it shapes our sense of killing. Once upon a time in battle films or massacre scenes you had to enlist and outfit extras—real bodies. That was expensive, even if sometimes a picture could rent some spare army from a peaceful nation. When David Selznick filmed the scenes of southern dead and wounded for *Gone With the Wind*, he had many real men feigning death and some fake bodies in the distance. Observers remarked that if the Confederacy had had that many living soldiers it would not have lost the war. There is a famous shot in that classic film where the craned camera roams over the open-air field hospital in Atlanta until it comes to the resplendent, tattered Confederate flag.

Much of that physical re-creation is now avoidable—or passed on to another department of moviemaking. This has reduced actuality or spatial immediacy in film. The laying in of what is a new kind of animation leaves less sense of responsibility or human damage. The computer can generate the living and the dead soldiery. There are technical geniuses who have made this possible (while undercutting the power of directors and actors). They have been servants and enablers in the cause of death and murder.

But if you grasp how technology can influence our ways of thinking and storytelling, consider that computer-generated masses are easier to hire and dispose of. We should use a lowercase h, but we have arrived at a potential holocaust of unknown and unknowable soldiers. And it follows that at a more personal level, we can now show the shattering of bodies without the laborious and complicated craft of makeup, prosthesis, and those inserted sachets of blood that exploded with an electrical impulse and made death lyrical for Sam Peckinpah and other directors.

A prettification has arrived in filmmaking that often eliminates the need to stage real events and to benefit from the imaginative involvement of human beings. The people in films have lost actuality, or vitality—is it a subtle retreat from life, all the more perilous for being unplanned?

So the numbering of the dead has become technical or clerical. Not that death and murder have stopped being treated because of that. But we need to keep a careful track of what is happening, instead of being monopolized or awestruck by big numbers alone. Let murder hold on to its drama—and melodrama.

Uncle Charlie tells a story when you visit him in his assisted living home. He yarns on about the Cossacks in 1945. Never heard of them? They were people who had quit the Soviet Union, some as early as the 1920s, some during the Second World War. They hated communism, and some of them fought on the German side in the second war. Then, at the Yalta conference in 1945, Churchill and Roosevelt signed off on the "repatriation" of those Cossacks to the Soviet Union once the war was over. There were 40,000 to 50,000 of them, and the repatriation was not optional.

No one had illusions about what was going to happen to those Cossacks. So truly, the local operatives in charge of them had to get out of their right mind—this is often necessary and you can call it prejudicial, a prelude to murder. The operatives told the

Cossacks on their word of honor that everything was going to be all right. No harm would befall them. But British soldiers sometimes had to beat the Cossacks trying to escape and throw them back on the trains or in the trucks to have them relocated to the east. That was the spring of 1945, in the elation of victory, and it was something held back from public knowledge.

Uncle Charlie also read the other day that academics who study such things estimate that, so far, about 106 billion people have lived on Earth. "That goes back to around 50,000 B.C.," he says. "I suppose before that we didn't exactly count as civilized. Anyway, every one of the 106 billion so far has died." He laughs that dying laugh.

The numbers are beyond grasp or an attempt at caring, but the predicament is consuming. Murder in the movies or in books is a kind of theatre meant to defy our own ordinary fate. That's the only way I can find of reconciling its hideous depiction and our reluctance to depart. That's how death can sometimes acquire a gallant comic flourish—Chaplin tried that with *Monsieur Verdoux* (1947), his attempt to play a serial killer. It didn't work at the box office as well as *Kind Hearts and Coronets*, but by then there were forces of righteousness suspicious of Charlie's way with young women and communist ideas, and ready to bring the wealthy tramp down.

Verdoux might have done better with Orson Welles in the lead, and Welles claimed that the idea for the picture had been his. If you feel Welles never got enough credit as an actor, just think of him as an overweight, loquacious charmer who keeps on killing wives and mistresses. In a way, that's the attitude he had as Harry Lime in *The Third Man*, looking down from the big wheel in the Prater at the humans far below, and chatting up Holly Martins:

> Would you really feel any pity if one of those dots stopped moving forever? If I said you can have twenty thousand pounds for every dot that stops, would you really, old man, tell me to keep my money . . . ?

The movies are wooed by serial killers. They always hope for some idea or character that clicks with the public so they can do it again and again. And if a murderer does his thing regularly (with dedication or persistence), doesn't that take the sting out of any particular killing? After all, serialization has been at the heart of film and television production, and in our nature as organisms. We're serial breathers, and devoted to so many other repetitions. Don't misunderstand this, but the more often a murderer murders the closer he (or she—though it's rarely she) comes to comedy or self-parody. Most habits become more neurotic and foolish the longer you look at them. The dead Michael Myers disappeared at the end of *Halloween* (1978) so he could come back for so many more films. Forty years later he's back again: Jamie Lee Curtis has grown older, but death is still fresh.

Sometimes a murderer does it just the once. In Michael Haneke's *Amour* (2012), Georges and Anne are a married couple in their eighties, the age of their players, Jean-Louis Trintignant and Emmanuelle Riva. They have lived on music and being music teachers; they are not the murderous type—they'd sooner listen to Schubert than read Agatha Christie or Simenon. But Anne falls ill and suffers paralysis. She has a stroke and begins to enter dementia. Georges will not put her into any other care but his own. One night he tells her a story about childhood and she seems to understand it. Then he takes a pillow and smothers her. It is murder, and a pained act of love and respect that has lived for life up until that last moment. There was a glimmer of smile on Jack Vincennes's face. He didn't want to go, and his going was rude and uncalled for. But he was amused to think he had expected anything else.

SOLITARY CONFINEMENT

In the age of computer-generated imagery, there are movie scientists who spend days and nights creating armies for a picture that will then be wiped out in some dawn of the dead. And there are cinephiles, or chronic movie watchers, who can recount the details of decimation and destruction with something like glee or innocence, as if no one had been hurt. If you've seen 100,000 screen deaths, when did the damage hurt? Or are the dead just extras, like the fleeting electronic figments from World of Warfare or whatever?

Accordingly, it is taken for granted now that movies are so violent that excess is overlooked. It is said that censorship has given up the ghost. I'm not sure that's true. Ratings are still applied and enforced. And this boastfully daring medium often flinches from its own legendary violence. At the end of the sixteenth century, Caravaggio painted *Judith Beheading Holofernes,* and that still moment stays breathtakingly immediate and un-ashamed. There's Judith; there's the knife; there's the victim's head with blood starting to spurt. Looking at the picture is like putting your finger in a power socket. We feel we are at or in slaughter. Movies are seldom that lucid or faithful to what happens in unedited coverage of severed heads. But they do glorify the expectation of violence. They hint at it, gloatingly—think of the ear about to be cut off in Quentin Tarantino's *Reservoir Dogs*—and make an anticipatory fetish of an action that will not be naked. They idolize damage more than they care to show it.

So when does a movie grasp its alleged pain, instead of offering a trigger function? Are we coroners in an archival morgue, or relatives who have lost our loved ones?

If it was six million in the Holocaust, can we feel every loss? Or do we have to yield to accepting all the deaths there have been, without mourning keeping us in night? (Can we make a pun about such a thing?)

On July 22, 2011, Anders Behring Breivik set off a homemade bomb in Oslo that killed eight people. He then went to the island of Utoya to the north of the city, pretending to be a policeman, and shot and killed sixty-nine young people gathered there at a Workers' League camp.

Breivik was thirty-two, the child of a broken home who had given signs of being disturbed early in life. It was said he had a fixed smile that seemed unrelated to external events. He had been a graffiti artist, and then a bodybuilder. He did well in school, despite his apparent aloneness. His state of mind made him unfit for military service, but he may have undergone paramilitary training in Belarus. The facts on that are unclear, but he liked to think of himself as a soldier. He had a computer programming business, but it was not a success. He purchased guns. He was running short of money. He had become hostile to Muslims and to feminism, and he believed the culture of Norway was going to hell.

Of course, you know some of this, along with a feeling that Breivik is unknowable. But he became a sensation in a few hours, and he is alive still in a prison in Skien, where he has a modest three-room suite, thanks to Norway's liberal regard for those in long-term incarceration. He was tried for murder and convicted and sentenced to twenty-one years (the most that Norway allows), but the state has the power to extend that sentence as it deems fit.

He is in solitary confinement, alone in his rooms, and it is said that he is writing.

So far, two movies have been made about that day. Do you want to see them—or question their necessity?

Utøya–July 22 is a film in Norwegian, by Erik Poppe, a dramatization of the action on the island. It premiered at the Berlin Film Festival in February 2018, and it is a study of the massacre conveyed in actual time. Breivik is no more than a distant figure. Poppe said his film was an attempt to portray the horror of right-wing terrorism as a warning to the world. But did the world need to be warned about the arbitrary slaughter of those kids? Did it require a lesson against massacre? Will the lesson work?

22 July appeared nine months later, and this was subtler and trickier to assess. It was written and directed by Paul Greengrass as an English-language drama. It concentrated on Breivik (played by Anders Danielsen Lie) and one of his victims, Viljar Hanssen (Jonas Strand Gravli), who was shot five times and then struggled to adapt to life with a lost eye and a shattered arm and leg, as well as the mental trauma, so that he could testify at Breivik's trial.

Greengrass shows the destruction (he directed *United 93* and several of the *Bourne* films—he has a rep with damage). We follow Viljar through surgeries and his agonized rehabilitation. On the island, we see the shooting and the implacable thoroughness of Breivik's task. We watch children hiding in fear—but being discovered by bullets. We look at Viljar's damaged face. And we are not called on to be nurses or comforters. Is the damage truly felt if we are so detached, and if we are helpless accomplices in the ruthless shooting? We may hate Breivik and what he did, but isn't there something compromising about his screened actions? Hasn't the technology of video combat games so affected our way of watching that responsiveness has been diminished or calmed?

22 July is more testing than even those questions. For as the film shows us Viljar's pain and courage, so it attends to Breivik's thought processes.

The first psychiatric examiner of the killer believed he was a paranoid schizophrenic. Under that diagnosis, his trial would have been a formality. But Breivik resisted that conclusion by mustering a willful intelligence that hardly seemed mad. He claimed to be a warrior in a just fight—the fascist opposition to all things that undermined Norwegian purity and cultural strength.

We may believe he is wrong, and deluded; but he is certain he is right, and he was shrewd about how he was perceived by the nation at large. And smart minds have a way of controlling movies. He says he was not mad, and he was sane enough to see how that point should be made clear to the public. He was determined to speak at his trial. He believed in a war that few others have joined or even noticed. He is opposed to the world. But is that necessarily insane? He knew exactly what he was doing. Many creative people feel not just that antagonism, but an inner conviction that they understand life better than others. It can be a radiant aloneness.

This presentation of Breivik is so arresting it makes us want more of him in the film. Lie is a brilliant player—as well as a qualified doctor: we may remember him as the haunted, suicidal character from Joachim Trier's *Oslo, 31 August*, where his pathos (not self-pity) was so compelling. But he does not have the shaved head or the empty stare that are so daunting in pictures of the real Breivik. Lie is so "good" or thoughtful we are led to feel how Breivik's mind is working. Moreover, actors are trained in wanting to please and persuade us—that pliancy is their calling, and it is a plea in their eyes that defies blankness, alienation, or the absence of thought. If actors do approach that nihilistic state it is by virtue of great pretending (think of Robert De Niro in *Taxi Driver*) so that the hideous extremity of a character can be sentimentalized or humanized by the actor's inventiveness.

The result is confusing. 22 *July* is well made. We feel we understand what happened; we like Viljar and loathe Breivik—but the pulse of movies, as we have seen, is strangely kind to villains and murderers.

I remain unsure why the film was made, or whether it should have been. In *Sight & Sound*, Nick James observed, "I wonder if now Breivik isn't quietly smiling to himself at the prospect of his message being presented to cinema."

That's a valid worry. 22 *July* gives Breivik a terrible warped dignity as well as a forum. I fear that the movie's austere demon could beckon other troubled loners with its helpless complacency. That is not just because of the arrangement of its narrative and the art of the acting. It is because film cannot show slaughter without cutting off the spectacle from felt damage. The murders become a kind of rite. No one doubts their horror— but why are we watching when we would not watch the willful slaughter of animals or the steady rape of children?

Damage needs to be protected as an outrage to life.

This matter of aloneness eats at me. A writer can say solitude is exemplary, yet a weakness; it may be a standard to maintain for observation and description, but it is also vanity and self-pity, like seeds in the dark.

I was talking with my son Zachary after we had seen *Joker* (2019), so boring but so piercing. I said that, had I been a distributor, I would have flinched from taking on *Joker* (even if I'd known its box office in advance). I would have wondered if its charismatic madman might not foster violence in some spectators out there alone as they were entranced by the Joker's crippled spider dance. But could my uneasiness be confined to just one film? Or isn't it the tropic air for all of them?

Zachary told me about "incels" (involuntary celibates, impacted loners) and their response to the film. We realize there are unaccountable victims of mental illness out there—or in here. I tried to explain a movie dilemma: raw surveillance of mad people teaches you that they are out of reach, utterly unglamorous. Whereas Joaquin Phoenix cannot help but be mesmerizing, a kind of wounded genius. Is he even a way of suggesting, isn't this now the desperate state of disaffection and solitude that can think of murder as a rite for actors?

AND NOW, DEATH

Do we cling to murder just because we are afraid of death, but too timid to admit that? Time and again in modern American cinema, the supposedly wholesome lives of citizens are threatened or overlooked by some Other apparition. Did it begin with *Night of the Living Dead* (1968)? Isn't it there in films as varied as Darren Aronofsky's *mother!* (2017) and Jordan Peele's *Us* (2019)? To say nothing of the vague but gathering menace of flawed lookalikes at the end of the street. Is that the homeless fueled by black magic or a rumor of cultural hostility?

But in the fear of fear we may forget to live, or honor life enough.

The other day, I came on something written by John Berger. He was noting the death of Tony Godwin, the publisher of *A Fortunate Man* (1967), the book about a country doctor that Berger made with photographer Jean Mohr. They had been friends and Godwin had encouraged that adventurous book. But Godwin had died suddenly in 1976. He had been the instrumental publisher at Penguin Books in the 1960s, my boss.

"Tony's life now belongs, historically, to the past," wrote Berger. "Physically his body, simplified by burning to the element of carbon, re-enters the physical process of the world. Carbon is the prerequisite for any form of life, the source of the organic. I tell myself these things not in order to concoct a specious alchemy of immortality, but in order to remind myself that it is my view of time which is being remorselessly cross-examined by death. There is no point in using death to simplify ourselves."

We must heed that advice: murder can be headlights in the night that turn us into deer. At seventy or so, we have likely witnessed in the region of 150,000 killings on our screens, like waves coming in on a beach. These events were frequently melodramatic or "exciting"; they involved drastic violence, and many of them were memorable, "stunning," and even beautiful. You've grown accustomed to this impact by now. Not that it always feels wondrous. To see the skin peeled off a living face is a test of the old insurance scheme, "It's only a movie." Some people who are easily shocked gave up going to the movies long ago. Not that I am opposed to schemes of lethal rapture.

Every time I see *The Conformist* (1970) I marvel at its lovely sequence in the woods. Then I wonder, is "lovely" too much? Clerici (Jean-Louis Trintignant), our hero, and Manganiello (Gastone Moschin), his domineering henchman, are tracking

Professor Quadri and his wife. Assassination is on the agenda: we know this, even the Quadris sense it—only Clerici clings to a cowardly hope that the worst may not happen.

We are in a dense forest on a deserted road in gloomy winter light. There is snow on the ground. An ambush stops the Quadri car up ahead—Clerici and Manganiello have been following behind the target car. Quadri is stabbed to death, many times, so many times—we see it from the horrified point of view of his wife, Anna (Dominique Sanda). She gets out of the car and runs back to Clerici's car for rescue. Not that she can trust mercy by then. But maybe the car holds passersby who are not part of the conspiracy. Still, running back to that car is a revelation as grim as murder, for she will discover that it is Clerici hunched in the back, the man she thought she might be in love with. So if she was going to betray her husband, her own forlorn romantic urge is now crushed. She screams and beats on the car window; he gazes at her, stricken, but as cold as the glass. She's only inches away, but he's sitting there alone in his room.

Anna is wearing a fashionable ivory-colored dress, so we can see her clearly as she runs off into the woods, desperate to escape. It's no use; we know that as the handheld camera pursuit bumps through the trees. Soon enough she is hit by a bullet; she staggers and turns, her face streaked in blood. It makes a beautiful scene—why not, with Bernardo Bertolucci directing, Vittorio Storaro doing the photography, and Nando Scarfiotti in charge of "design"? That triumvirate were a last peak of classical cinema—of photographing people in space, with real events being seen and felt in a ravishing design. It's murder as a kind of ecstasy, and the music by Georges Delerue brims with regret.

I'm not ashamed of admitting the enchantment of this scene, the numbness of Trintignant (decades before he made *Amour*), and the heartbreaking elegance of Dominique Sanda—she was not a particularly good actress, but she was a figurehead in the era when cinema was often a matter of beautiful women being stripped or murdered, or both.

Does this great sequence teach us that murder is "wrong"? Didn't we know that already? Or is its cinematic grace a test of what we are supposed to know and feel?

The early 1970s were a summit in film history (there seemed so many masterpieces in that age). And it's not that screen killing has subsided. Murder rates in life are falling, but the realized fantasy is a screen tsunami now, as if CGI massacres and their liberated indifference have taken on the dynamic evident in the 1940s and 1950s in the Tom and Jerry cartoons, where the valiant cat (he only wanted to eat a mouse) was flattened, cooked, electrocuted, smithereened, vaporized (whatever) so that he could be instantly reassembled—in order that he might be massacred again.

As the impetus of movie potency shifted from "cinema" to long-form television series, there were exceptional shows, like *Breaking Bad* (2008–13), in which a regular, decent, failing American—a family man and a high school teacher, Walter White (Bryan Cranston)—learns he has cancer and so cancels his conventional deal with getting along as best he can. It's crime now for him. Instead of school-level chemistry, he'll become a drugs factory. And people will die because of it.

So much murder—so little death.

By which I mean to ask how often have you encountered the real thing; in all those spectacular set pieces have you witnessed real death, as in the departure of life, as opposed to murder in a story? That thickening reality is delivered occasionally on screen with helpless simplicity. Near the end of Peter Weir's neglected *The Way Back* (2010), a girl, Irena, played by Saoirse Ronan, expires. She had joined a few men—thousands of miles ago, as they tried to walk from gulag imprisonment in Siberia in 1943 . . . walking to wherever they could be safe, out of the Soviet Union, through Mongolia and China, and eventually to India.

This girl had attached herself to the group; she told lies about who she was; but along the way an older man (Ed Harris), looking like worn leather, had got the truth out of her and become like a grudging father. They had walked so far, across the Gobi Desert, and she had been depleted. In the desert light, and with Ms. Ronan's natural paleness and sparseness, there was a sense of her life being erased. Her face was burned from the sun, and at last she lay down and stopped breathing. That is how we do it; it's how most of us will die. But it's the sort of scene you don't see too much on screens, as if to say, aren't those sprightly, colorful, instant murders meant to take our minds off where we're going?

Death arrived as an arresting spokesman on film in 1957. On a black and white pebbled beach in Ingmar Bergman's *The Sev-*

enth Seal he appeared as a character. As played by Bengt Ekerot in a makeup white face and in a black shroud that exposed only the face, this upright Death was like a chess piece. That was appropriate because the knight (Max von Sydow, aged twenty-eight) was playing a game with himself. So Death told him, Now, I am here to take you. We will play chess and if you can beat me or hold me off you have a little longer—as long as the film runs (96 minutes). It was Bobby Fischer who would say that chess was about destroying your opponent.

Bergman was preoccupied with death, but I can't think of many murders or killings in his work. (*The Virgin Spring* has a few, but they're awkward, as if he didn't know how to film them.) Instead, who can forget the slow, tender death of Agatha (Harriet Andersson) in *Cries and Whispers*, wearing white in a scarlet room, from uterine cancer—and that was only twenty years after Andersson had been the naked Monika, a vibrant glimpse of a new cinematic sexuality, in *Summer with Monika* (1953).

That 1957 Death was a portentous, theatrical character, for Bergman loved theatre as much as film, and nursed a melodramatic sense of his own struggle in life. But in the shadow of death he wasn't drawn to do murder in his films—so *Cries and Whispers* is as much a treasure of 1972 as *The Godfather*, and a superior work. Even dressed up in black, that Death was a reminder of the plain thing. But a little overdone, or solemn. In a Preston Sturges version of *The Seventh Seal* (just imagine that), Death might have worn a fashionable blazer and been witty, polite, and rather silly—I see Rudy Vallee in the part, selling real estate packages in Florida. That's the kind of Death agent we deserve now.

And in the total casualty list of life—that 106 billion, if you recall—the majority have died or passed away quietly, alone— it has to be done alone, no matter the fond company that has gathered—and they were not shot or knived, not obliterated by death rays or devoured by dragons. Their cause of death was stroke, heart failure, pneumonia, some cancer, a tumor here or there, or simply exhaustion. It was matter-of-fact and it never made the movies. It was biological, organic, in the nature of things. Very little really happened except inertia.

But so much happens in time's overlapping that doesn't get into movies. The most striking film I saw in the moment of the shootings at Santa Fe High School near Houston was *Vertigo Sea*. This is a simultaneous performance of 43 minutes on three side-by-side video screens. I saw it at the San Francisco Museum of Modern Art with my daughter Kate, and we stumbled by chance into the long dark room where it was playing. We had not heard about it in advance and we sat there watching, feeling happy, I think, at being moved by it together. Did we feel specially alive?

Vertigo Sea is a movie—I want to call it that—assembled by John Akomfrah. The pervasive element in the three screens is the ocean, and there is ravishing footage of seas stretched out for us, tranquil and in turmoil, such a source of momentousness and wonder, and yet so dangerous or so much larger than humans. On a few viewings of *Vertigo Sea*, I'm not sure how premeditated or organized the show is, or how far the three screens are meant to "fit together." There are affinities, to be sure. But I think Akomfrah's hope is to set up many fluent associations, half-heard rhymes, or crossed references. In the museum space, you can't see or register everything. You feel you're seeing an attempt at a play, but in a large public space where so many other things are going on. So meaning becomes variable and not a unique sharp point.

Vertigo Sea has several motifs like waves, coming and coming again—our slaughter of whales and polar bears; the trade in slavery; the travails of boat people; and the adventure and the peril in going to sea. There is a mixture of very old footage—documentary or newsreel—with handsome, surreal inventions that involve figures, often in period costume, on shorelines, looking out at the sea waiting for some significance to appear in Death, or Life.

That enigma is central. We live now in a culture that is gossiping over the Death of the Planet. I don't mean to minimize that threat, or save us from it—I believe in the future legend of global warming and all the ways we have offended nature. But one lesson of *Vertigo Sea* is that the Earth will not die. It may rid itself of human existence—all in one go, like a dog shaking off rain, or gradually, like cell life forming. But the Earth will not notice that or grieve. We will persist, if only as carbon (call it C). In watching *Vertigo Sea* one is distressed by polar bears being shot and killed, or the humiliation of whales as some rusted harpoon anchors them and begins to flood the sea with their blood. But that anguish is in our looking—films are wondrous or tragic only because we are there to watch them. And we are the only species that can observe our own cruelty and destiny as fit for grandeur or tragedy instead of the repetition of waves.

The oceans are sublime, or beyond humanity—they will carry on if no manned boats sail on them, or if the oceans rush through the subway system of New York and clean up those streets for good. It was Travis Bickle who promised, "Someday a *real* rain will come and wash all the scum off the streets."

As far as we know anything, we trust that in the cellular scum of marine life our existence began and may be regenerated if the need arises. It is blind, deaf, and indifferent. It soars above understanding. And I am not referring to God; I mean the perpetuity that we sometimes call "science," or organic evolution. I remember an episode of a television series, *The Ascent of Man* (1973), where its on-camera host, Jacob Bronowski, picked up handfuls of soil from a burial ground at Auschwitz and talked about how life would come back from that shocked earth.

At least, that's what he said to the best of my memory. But our precious memories are just bubbles in the Pacific.

I am not sure now of the year, but I think it was 1958. My maternal grandfather was named Herbert George Moore. I would suppose that he was in his late seventies by then, and I was sixteen. He had been ill in recent years. He had cancer of the larynx and trachea; that had led to an operation after which he breathed through a tube that emerged in his throat. He could speak only in whispered air. It was not easy talking with him, but I would go over to his house about four miles from where I lived—from Streatham to Hackbridge on the southern edge of London— and we would listen to music together. He was a kind man, who loved card games and the horses—he took me once to Epsom for a day at the races.

What I recall now is my wish to convince him that I loved him and wanted to talk with him. But he only smiled, as if to tell me that that was not quite possible by then. In how many situations do we smile at one another as if to forgive the inexpressible? The helplessness can be more life-affirming than a "Yes!" or a kiss. Sometimes you can look at your dog and wonder if it is smiling.

I was told he might be dying. So one summer afternoon I rode over on my bike to see him. My grandma welcomed me and asked me to stay quiet. "Bert"—that's how everyone spoke of him—was not well. He was in the garden. He was sitting there alone in his shirtsleeves in the sun. I thought he was asleep.

He had died. I know so little about him. He was my grandfather, but he was a bubble, too. I imagine he was born in about 1880. He had a job as a clerk in the City of London, a humble position. I don't think he had been in school past sixteen. He had not served in the Great War because he had a withered arm, or an arm in which he had reduced movement. He had a wife and two daughters, and my mother adored him while admitting rather proudly that he had had what was called an eye for the ladies that might have spurred my grandmother's famous temper.

I do not know who Bert's father was, but that man might have been born around 1850, as photography came into our lives. In the same way, I do not know who my great-grandchildren will be—though I may get to see some of them. Or not. Our lives and destinies can seem so important—so deserving of great murders—but history's tidal rhythm will slip over all of them and make for oblivion. And in half a dozen generations it may be that oblivion or the erosion of being human has grown in us so much that murder is more comfortable, or less noticeable.

As I write this (October 2018), much of the world is outraged because a Saudi writer went into the Saudi Arabian embassy in Istanbul, seeking papers to assist in his divorce. He was never seen again by his fiancée. There are reports that he was murdered in the embassy, that his body was cut up with a bone saw, and the parts scattered who knows where? This is horrific and should not be forgotten. But do you recall his name?

Bert was sitting in his chair and his head was tipped down on his chest, but there was no sign of distress or pain or even regret. I think he may have been asleep when he died, for his eyes were closed. In that state—this may be just the overlook of wishful thinking—I thought there was the ghost of a smile on his face. Perhaps that is how I care to think of it now, as if there might be smilelike shapes in a face after life has moved on. I think I am the only person left sixty years later who could remember him or the small jewels of my childhood with Bert and Grandma: a hot-water bottle made of porcelain; hard-boiled egg sandwiches on new bread cut so thin you could see the shadow of the knife through it; the smell of tobacco that clung to Bert as he taught me cribbage.

I did not know the official cause of his death. Or the buried hopes of his life. We took no photograph of him in his chair. I think that would have felt indecent then. But not now? In our feeble fitful ways, we change, or we let time pass through us, and think things are getting better or worse. Grandma put a white cloth over his face and I lay on the ground in the garden until people came to carry him away. Then I lifted up his chair and put it back in the house. There was birdsong in the late afternoon.

It is only now, remembering his death, that I realize this common man, without special education or opportunity, had two daughters in the years before the Great War and named them Nora and Trilby. My mother told me she thought she was Nora after the young wife in Ibsen's *A Doll's House* (which first played in London in 1884), while Trilby must nod to the George du Maurier novel, published in 1894. Not that either sister escaped her house, but suppose he thought of that possibility for them.

So Herbert George Moore had read that book or seen that play? I think so, though I had not appreciated that before. He had chosen names that might have been glaring or comic at his level of society, and that must mean he had such hope for his daughters.

"I've put the eggs on," said my grandmother, and very soon I saw the gray of her knife carving thin slices for our sandwiches. We were hungry, or she was saying that need was natural at a death. And now, I try to restore Bert's liveliness or amend his solitude. He is there still.

"There you are, young man." She gave me the warm sandwich on a plate. The yolk was soaking in the bread.

SOURCES AND THANKS

Tooting Bec Common was my adventure playground from the moment Grannie told me in the spring of 1945 that Hitler might be hiding there. This was in his brief moment of being a missing person. I looked but did not find his cruel mustache in the undergrowth. But a few years later there was a story about a prostitute's corpse in one of the less penetrable wooded parts of the Common. Then there was the Priory and the story of Charles Bravo.

The Priory was a grand house on the Balham side of the Common, and my family told me (with local pride) that it was where Charles Bravo, a successful lawyer, had been found in 1876, poisoned. No one was ever charged in the case and rumor had shuffled suicide, accident, and murder in endless enigma. Murders are all very well; and big-house English murders have few rivals; but murders without answer never lose their charm.

And if we want them to stay unsolved, isn't that a sign of furtive sympathy?

I know the Bravo story infected me—and others. The lawyer had passed a couple of days dying, and said nothing. There was a novel prompted by the case, *For Her to See* (it was by the fecund but mysterious Marjorie Bowen under one of her pen names), and it led to a film called *So Evil My Love* (1948)—there are movie titles that live in a separate state of myth, hardly needing a movie. "So Evil My Love" is endlessly provocative in its marriage of the desirable and the horrid (it could have served for this book). Ann Todd starred in the movie, and years later I was talking to her (about David Selznick), and I remarked on how much I had liked her in *Madeleine* (see p. 151), where she plays a likely poisoner. She nodded in a rather vexed way—she was lovely, but as if made of porcelain—and said she didn't understand how she had ended up playing a couple of "bad lots." But devotees of nice English murders know that the bad lot is like the top hat or the iron in Monopoly. You can't play without them.

So I thank Ann Todd, as well as Janet Leigh, who chatted in an amusing way about being a patient victim in a shower for a week, for Hitchcock. No one writing about film has escaped Hitchcock's shadow or his lethal grace. Anyone English feels the half-indecent attraction he had towards terrible things, presented as if perfect. And if I have been tough on David Fincher in this book, I thank him now for his disturbing films.

Steve Wasserman took on this book at Yale University Press when he was an editor there, and I remember conversations where we marveled that highly educated, politically correct chumps (like ourselves) had murderous minds on our sofas with everything from *The Sopranos* to *Peaky Blinders*. Were we part of those gangs? After Steve moved on, the defense of the book was maintained at Yale by John Donatich and Sarah Miller, and I am grateful to both of them. After that I fell into the last clutches of Dan Heaton (he is retiring?), one of the best text editors I have been lucky enough to work with. My thanks also go to Phillip King, to Ash Lago, and to Nancy Ovedovitz for a jacket design that exactly understood my dreams.

Beyond them I had valuable readings from Michael Ondaatje and Richard Burt, and I owe them plenty for their insights and their delighted but sometimes dismayed advice. Why not? Murder should be upsetting. Without that it risks becoming a mere habit.

But I realize, all the time, that thinking about murder began as a family pastime. So my parents and grandparents (who all figure in the book) were accomplices. The book is dedicated to Kate, my eldest daughter, and a steady warning and inspiration. But there is room too to thank her siblings, Mathew, Rachel (for one blissful June afternoon in Virginia Woolf's garden at Rodmell), Nicholas, and Zachary. As well as Anne and Lucy— who is a voice in the book and my fellow-watcher.

INDEX

Index